Classic
POTATO DISHES

Classic POTATO DISHES

Sue Ashworth • Carol Handslip • Jane Hartshorn
Kathryn Hawkins • Wendy Lee • Cara Hobday • Louise Steele
Rosemary Wadey • Pamela Westland

SMITHMARK

This edition published in the USA in 1996 by SMITHMARK Publishers,
a division of U.S. Media Holdings Inc.,
16, East 32nd Street, New York, NY 10016

First published in the UK in 1996

SMITHMARK books are available for bulk purchase for sales promotion and premium
use. For details write or call the manager of special sales, SMITHMARK Publishers,
16 East 32nd Street, New York, NY 10016; (212) 532-6800

ISBN: 0-765-19864-9

Produced by Haldane Mason, London

Acknowledgements
Editor: Lisa Dyer
Design: Digital Artworks Partnership Ltd
Photography: Karl Adamson, Sue Atkinson, Iain Bagwell, Martin Brigdale,
Amanda Heywood, Joff Lee, Patrick McLeavey and Clive Streeter
Home Economists: Sue Ashworth, Carole Handslip, Jane Hartshorn, Kathryn Hawkins,
Cara Hobday, Wendy Lee, Louise Steele, Rosemary Wadey, Pamela Westland

Printed in Italy

Material in this book has previously appeared in *Balti Cooking, Barbecues, Caribbean Cooking,
Cooking for One & Two, Cooking On A Budget, Indian Side Dishes, Indian Vegetarian Cooking,
Italian Regional Cooking, Low-fat Cooking, Mexican, Microwave Meals, Pasta Cooking, Picnics,
Pizza, Quick & Easy Indian Cooking, Quick & Easy Meals, Recipes with Yogurt, Sensational Salads,
Soups & Broths, Vegetarian Barbecues, Vegetarian Main Meals.*

Note:
Cup measurements in this book are for American cups.
Tablespoons are assumed to be 15ml. Unless otherwise stated, milk is assumed to be full-
fat, eggs are standard size 2 and pepper is freshly ground black pepper.

CONTENTS

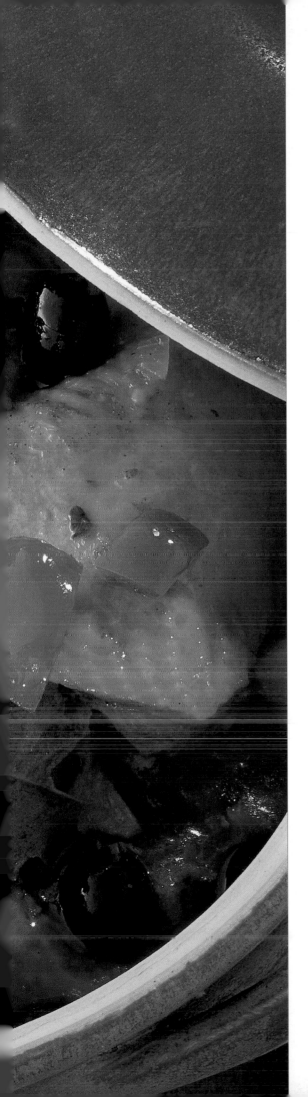

INTRODUCTION

One of the best qualities of the potato is that it tastes delicious with many other ingredients, spices and herbs, happily marrying flavors to produce dishes with entirely different characteristics. As a result, many cuisines contain dozens of potato recipes—in French cookery, for example, you would find literally hundreds of potato dishes. On the following pages, you will find some of the best French recipes, along with a diverse selection from countries around the world. You will also find recipes suitable for all occasions, from soups, salads, snacks, light meals, and side dishes, through to main meals, pies, and bakes. Classic favorites, such as Potatoes Lyonnaise, are featured, along with some inspired new creations, such as filled tortillas, Cornish pasties, and samosas.

Potatoes are an integral part of everyday cooking. Although we tend to think of the potato as everyday and native to America, it was actually a native plant of Ecuador, where it was discovered by the invading Spaniards around 1550. It was known as the *batata* or *battato,* and it is thought that early settlers in America traded with the Spaniards for it. It was not until Sir Walter Raleigh's expedition of 1584 that the potato was brought to Europe. At that time, the potato was regarded as a delicacy, and it wasn't until the eighteenth century that the potato firmly established as a crop in America.

The nutritional benefits of the potato are highly regarded. With today's emphasis on healthy eating, the potato has come into its own as a natural, wholesome food. Essentially a complex carbohydrate or "starchy" food, potatoes supply our bodies with an important source of energy. Starchy foods are now rightly regarded as an essential element of a healthy, well-balanced diet, and they should form a high proportion of our food intake. Not only do potatoes supply us with energy, they are also a useful source of vitamins and fiber, too. All potatoes supply fiber, especially in the skins, and potatoes also contain vitamin C and B_6, along with niacin, riboflavin, thiamin, and such minerals as copper, iron, magnesium, potassium, phosphorus, and zinc. Sweet potatoes are also very nutritious, containing vitamin A, calcium, iron, niacin, and potassium.

All aspects of potato cuisine are covered in this comprehensive cook book. If you are looking for a potato recipe to accompany a special meal, or if you just want inspiration for some tasty snacks, then you will find what you are looking for within these pages. The simple, step-by-step instructions will guide you through each recipe—so whether you are a culinary whiz in the kitchen or a novice cook, the results will be every bit as tasty!

SELECTING AND STORING POTATOES

The best rule for new-season potatoes is to buy them in small quantities when you need them. Try to use them within a day or two of purchase to enjoy their flavor at its best. Any damp soil sticking to the skin is a sure sign of freshness, and the skins themselves should rub away easily. Discard any potatoes that are showing a tendency to turn green—this is caused by exposure to light, and these potatoes should not be eaten.
Main-crop potatoes should be free from damage, dirt, and growth shoots. Again, avoid any potatoes with green discoloration. Choose those in good shape and buy in bulk if you have enough storage space available.
For small amounts of potatoes, keep them on a rack in a cool, dark place. If you have bought them in a plastic bag, empty them out, because the moisture that can form within the bag can cause the potatoes to rot. Brown paper bags are ideal for storage.
Remember to handle potatoes carefully because they can bruise easily, especially sweet potatoes. Keep in mind that warmth causes potatoes to sprout, damp makes them rot, and light turns them green; so a cool, dry, dark place that is free from frost is the ideal spot. If you have bought a sack of main-crop potatoes, keep it raised from the ground so air can circulate. Avoid keeping any potatoes close to strong-smelling foods, such as onions, which could taint their flavor.
If properly stored, new potatoes or thin-skinned boiling potatoes will keep for about two weeks, while baking or sweet potatoes keep for up to six months. Cooked potatoes will keep for up to three days in the refrigerator, while sweet potatoes should still be alright for up to a week after cooking. Mashed or puréed cooked potatoes can be frozen for two or three months, but do not freeze raw potatoes because they loose their firmness and texture.

THE PICK OF THE CROP

You may think that all potatoes will do the same job, and to some extent you would be right, but you wouldn't be getting the best from them! Different varieties have their own characteristics, and each is suited to a particular use. Thankfully, you don't have to become acquainted with all the many different potato varieties to know which purpose they are best suited to—in supermarkets and at market stalls, you will find some guidance on the potatoes' labeling and packaging to show the best way to use that specific variety. The package should indicate if a potato is suited to baking, mashing, roasting, or for making French fries. However, if the potatoes are sold loose, then you will need to ask the vendor or the supermarket manager for guidance.
The colorful names of potato varieties are increasingly referred to, meaning that you can quickly identify a potato for a particular purpose. Ask for the potatoes by these names when you b respected in any store!
Each type of potato can have different varieties of texture, from floury or mealy to creamy or waxy, meaning that they lend themselves to different treatments. Usually floury potatoes, which describes the texture after cooking, means it is a baking potato, and a waxy potato will indicate a boiling potato. You will find some that are good all-rounders, suitable for many purposes, though you may like to try a wide range to pinpoint your preferences. The size of potatoes can vary enormously, from tiny ones weighing less than ½ ounce to huge ones weighing in at 1 pound or more. Here is a round-up of some of the more popular varieties:

Alcmaria This variety is suitable for all-round use, though especially good in potato salads.

Arran Pilot Because these potatoes keep their shape well, they are excellent in potato salads.

Belle de Fontenay With a pale yellow skin and yellow flesh, these potatoes are excellent when boiled or steamed and served in salads or stews.

Blue The blue varieties, such as Blue Carib and All Blue, have a grayish blue skin and a blue flesh. They have a subtle flavor that is best enjoyed when simply boiled.

Cara This is a large, round main-crop potato, suitable for all uses, though especially good for baking.

Catriona A yellow-skinned variety with cream-colored flesh, it has a delicious flavor and a floury texture. Steam, bake, or roast this type.

Desirée This is a good, all-round variety with red skin and pale yellow flesh.

Estima Another all-purpose variety, this attractive potato has pale yellow skin and flesh, and an even, oval shape.

Epicure This variety has white-fleshed skin with a pink tinge and a creamy flesh that has very good flavor. It is excellent in salads, but also good for boiling and mashing.

Finnish Yellow Waxed A yellow-fleshed variety which is great for potato salads or boiled in the skin.

German Fingerling A small, light-skinned potato with a yellow flesh. It is best simply boiled.

Idaho Also called Russet potatoes, which includes such varieties as Russet Burbank and Butte. This favorite is a baking potato with reddish brown skin. It is known as an Idaho even though it is produced in other states.

King Edward A main-crop variety with creamy-colored flesh, suitable for all-round use.

Maris Bard This is an early-season potato variety with good cooking qualities. It has white skin and flesh.

Maris Piper A main-crop potato variety with a white skin and creamy-colored flesh. This is an excellent all-rounder, especially good for boiling, mashing, baking, and roasting.

Pentland Dell A popular main-crop potato with a long oval shape and creamy white flesh with a white skin. It is suitable for French fries, baking, mashing, and roasting.

Pentland Javelin A potato with excellent cooking qualities and a very white skin and flesh. Look for it after the first early potatoes have appeared.

Pentland Squire A perfect choice for baking or mashing, because of its floury texture. This is a white-skinned, white-fleshed variety, although it can occasionally have a russet appearance.

Pink Fir Apple This main-crop potato has the characteristics of new potatoes. It has excellent flavor and is particularly good in salads. It is a long, slightly knobbly potato with a pink flesh, and it has a firm, waxy texture.

Red Pontiac A variety with a dry, floury texture. It is often sold as new or boiling potatoes and is best when boiled.

Romano This red-skinned variety has a creamy flesh and is a good main-crop choice.

Rose Fir A small, waxy potato with a pink to red skin and a creamy consistency. It is best boiled.

White Rose A long, white, waxy variety, which is suitable for boiling, but may also be baked or made into French fries.

Wilja A good basic variety with all-round use. It has a yellow skin with a netted appearance and a pale yellow flesh. It is very useful for boiling and steaming, and for using in salads and casseroles, because it keeps its shape during cooking.

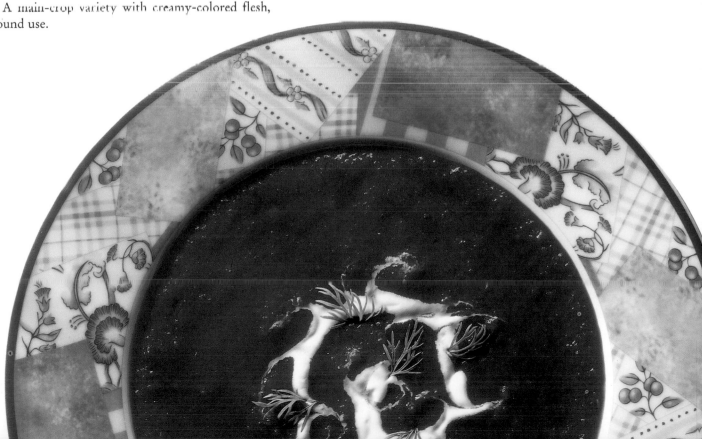

PREPARING AND COOKING POTATOES

Cut out eyes, sprouts, or any discolored areas. Use a potato peeler or proper peeling knife to peel potatoes, so you can peel them very thinly. Thick peeling is wasteful, as many of the nutrients are contained close to the skin. You will need to rinse them well after peeling and pat them dry with paper towels or a clean dish cloth. You can make french fries with unpeeled potatoes, which is a good way to conserve more nutrients; just scrub the potatoes very thoroughly, in the same way that you would prepare new potatoes.

To boil potatoes, cut them into even-sized pieces so they all cook evenly at the same time, put them into cold water in a saucepan, add a little salt if you wish, and bring up to a boil. Then cover, reduce the heat, and simmer slowly until the potatoes are tender. Serve immediately to prevent the potatoes from breaking up. Potatoes that are kept hot for a long period of time will lose more nutrients. Mashed potatoes make a warm, comforting dish in the winter months. Just mash boiled potatoes with a fork or potato masher, then add butter and milk and beat until light with a wooden spoon—or use a hand-held electric mixer to beater. Season with salt, pepper, and a little freshly ground nutmeg, if you like.

Baked potatoes are the easiest to prepare. Choose large, even-sized potatoes, free from blemishes. Scrub them well, cut out any damaged or discolored areas or eyes, and prick several times with a fork. Place the potatoes on a baking sheet and bake at 425°F for 1–1½ hours, until soft. You can bake them in a microwave oven if you prefer, although they won't have the same crispy skin. One large potato will take about 8 minutes. Remember to prick the skin first and turn the potato once halfway through the cooking time. Times will vary according to the size of potato, the number you are cooking, and the power of your microwave.

For roast potatoes, cut peeled potatoes into even-size pieces. Parboil them for 10 minutes to reduce the overall cooking time, or just roast them from raw if you prefer. To cook them, place the potatoes in a large roasting pan with some hot fat and bake at 450°F for 40 minutes to an hour before removing. You may like to coat the potatoes in flour before adding them to the hot fat. Larger roast potatoes will absorb less fat, and will therefore have a slightly lower calorie content. The same principle applies to french fries— large, straight-cut potatoes will absorb less fat, and have less calories, than smaller, crinkle-cut ones.

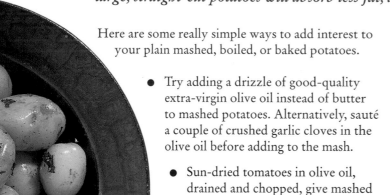

Here are some really simple ways to add interest to your plain mashed, boiled, or baked potatoes.

- Try adding a drizzle of good-quality extra-virgin olive oil instead of butter to mashed potatoes. Alternatively, sauté a couple of crushed garlic cloves in the olive oil before adding to the mash.

- Sun-dried tomatoes in olive oil, drained and chopped, give mashed potatoes an Italian slant. You may like to add some chopped fresh oregano or basil, too.

- Sauté a small onion in butter until golden, and stir it through mashed potatoes with plenty of ground black pepper and some Parmesan cheese. Pile the potatoes into an ovenproof serving dish, top with grated cheddar cheese, and grill until bubbling.

- Mix canned tuna fish that has been drained and flaked with chopped onion, canned corn kernels, and chopped red or green bell pepper. Dress it with a little olive oil and vinegar, and use to top baked potatoes.

- Combine chopped roast chicken, chopped scallions, and mayonnaise to taste. Use to top baked potatoes.

- Combine chopped cooked chicken or turkey with mayonnaise, flavor it with mild curry powder, and use to top baked potatoes.

- Combine soft cheese with grated cheddar cheese, a little chopped scallion, and some snipped chives. Use to top baked potatoes.

- Mix cooked peeled shrimp in a couple of tablespoons of commercially prepared seafood sauce and use to top baked potatoes.

- Sauté snipped bacon, chopped onion, and red bell pepper in butter, and use to top baked potatoes.

- Mix chopped cooked ham with cottage cheese and pineapple. Use to top baked potatoes.

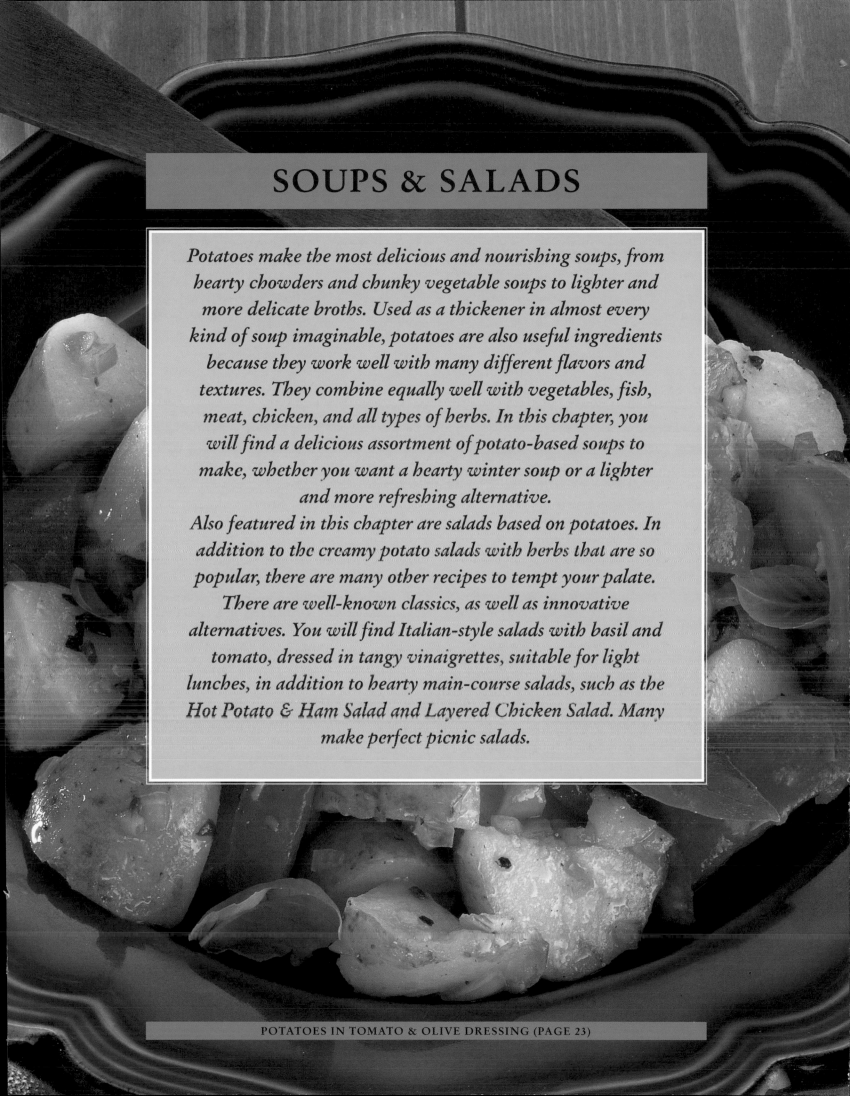

SOUPS & SALADS

Potatoes make the most delicious and nourishing soups, from hearty chowders and chunky vegetable soups to lighter and more delicate broths. Used as a thickener in almost every kind of soup imaginable, potatoes are also useful ingredients because they work well with many different flavors and textures. They combine equally well with vegetables, fish, meat, chicken, and all types of herbs. In this chapter, you will find a delicious assortment of potato-based soups to make, whether you want a hearty winter soup or a lighter and more refreshing alternative.

Also featured in this chapter are salads based on potatoes. In addition to the creamy potato salads with herbs that are so popular, there are many other recipes to tempt your palate. There are well-known classics, as well as innovative alternatives. You will find Italian-style salads with basil and tomato, dressed in tangy vinaigrettes, suitable for light lunches, in addition to hearty main-course salads, such as the Hot Potato & Ham Salad and Layered Chicken Salad. Many make perfect picnic salads.

POTATOES IN TOMATO & OLIVE DRESSING (PAGE 23)

FISH & SEAFOOD CHOWDER

Served with warm, crusty bread and a salad, this tasty soup makes a substantial lunch or supper dish.

SERVES 4

INGREDIENTS:
2 pounds mussels in their shells
1 large onion, thinly sliced
2 garlic cloves, chopped
3 bay leaves
few sprigs fresh parsley
few sprigs fresh thyme
1¼ cups water
8 ounces smoked haddock fillets
1 pound potatoes, peeled and diced
4 celery stalks, thickly sliced
8-ounce can corn kernels, drained and rinsed
⅔ cup plain yogurt
1 tsp cornstarch
⅔ cup dry white wine
¼ tsp chili powder, or to taste
pepper
2 tbsp chopped fresh parsley

1 ▼ Scrub the mussels, pull off the "beards" and rinse in several changes of cold water. Discard any open shells that remain open when tapped.

2 Put the onion, garlic, bay leaves, parsley. and thyme in a large saucepan and pour on the water. Add the mussels, cover, and cook over a high heat for 5 minutes, shaking the pan once or twice.

3 ▼ Line a colander with cheesecloth and place it in a bowl. Strain the mussel liquid into the bowl. Remove and shell the mussels, and set them aside. Discard the vegetables and herbs, and reserve the liquid.

4 ▲ Put the haddock, potatoes, and celery into the rinsed saucepan, add

2½ cups of cold water, and bring to a boil. Cover the pan and simmer for 10 minutes. Remove the haddock with a slotted spatula and skin, bone, and flake it. Remove the vegetables with a slotted spoon and strain the liquid into the reserved seafood liquid.

5 Return the cooking liquid to the rinsed saucepan, add the corn, and bring to a boil. Stir together the yogurt and cornstarch to make a smooth paste. Stir in a little of the fish liquid, then pour it into the pan. Stir until the yogurt is well blended, then add the reserved mussels, haddock, potatoes, and celery.

6 Add the white wine, season with chili powder and pepper, and heat the soup gently, without boiling. Taste and adjust the seasoning, if necessary.

7 Transfer to a warm serving dish and sprinkle with the chopped parsley. Serve hot.

SMOKED FISH CHOWDER

A really substantial soup with a subtle smoky flavor and chunky with vegetables and fish.

SERVES 4

INGREDIENTS:
¾ cup chopped bacon
1 lb potatoes, diced finely
2½ cups milk
1 fresh bay leaf
14-ounce can corn kernels,
 drained
12 ounces thin fillet smoked haddock
 or cod, skinned
4 scallions, white and green parts sliced
 thinly
salt and pepper
crusty bread, to serve

1 ▼ Fry the bacon in a saucepan for 2 minutes, then add the potatoes, milk, bay leaf, and seasoning. Bring to a boil and simmer for 5 minutes.

2 ▼ Add the corn, fish, and scallions, and cook for 5 minutes more.

3 Use 2 forks to break the fish into large flakes.

4 ▼ Turn the soup into a large soup tureen, or individual bowls, and serve with chunks of crusty bread.

SAGE & ONION CHOWDER

This thick, creamy onion soup, with plenty of fragrant fresh sage, is chock-full of chopped bacon, potatoes, and corn.

SERVES 4–6

INGREDIENTS:
¼ cup butter or margarine
4 onions, sliced very thinly or chopped
1–2 garlic cloves, crushed
4 slices lean bacon, chopped
2 tbsp all-purpose flour
3¼ cups fresh chicken or vegetable stock
1 pound potatoes, diced very finely
⅔ cup whole milk
about 7-ounce can corn kernels, well drained
1 tbsp chopped fresh sage, or 1½ tsp dried sage
2 tbsp white wine vinegar
salt and pepper
sprigs of fresh sage, to garnish
warmed bread, to serve

1 ▼ Melt the butter or margarine in a large saucepan, and gently sauté the onions and garlic for about 15 minutes, until soft but not colored.

2 Add the chopped bacon and continue to fry for a few minutes, allowing the onions to color a little. Stir in the flour and cook for another minute or so.

3 ▼ Add the chicken or vegetable stock and bring to a boil. Add the potatoes and seasoning, and simmer gently for 20 minutes.

4 ▼ Add the whole milk and corn and bring the soup back to a boil, then add the sage and vinegar and simmer for 10–15 minutes more, until the potatoes are very tender but not broken up.

5 Adjust the seasoning, garnish with sprigs of sage ,and serve while hot with warmed bread.

LEEK, POTATO, & CARROT SOUP

A quick, chunky soup, ideal for a snack or lunch. The leftovers can be blended to make one portion of creamed soup for the next day.

SERVES 2

INGREDIENTS:
1 leek, about 6 oz in weight
1 tbsp oil
1 garlic clove, crushed
3 cups fresh chicken or vegetable
*   stock*
1 bay leaf
¼ tsp ground cumin
1 cup diced potatoes
1 cup coarsely grated carrot
salt and pepper
chopped fresh parsley,
*   to garnish*

PUREED SOUP:
5 6 tbsp milk
1–2 tbsp heavy cream, crème fraîche,
*   or sour cream*

1 ▼ Trim off some of the coarse green part of the leek, then slice thinly and rinse in cold water. Drain well.

2 Heat the oil in a saucepan, add the leek and garlic, and fry gently for 2–3 minutes, until soft but barely colored. Add the stock, bay leaf, cumin, and seasoning, and bring to a boil.

3 Add the diced potato to the saucepan, cover, and simmer gently for 10–15 minutes, until the potato is just tender but not broken up.

4 ▼ Add the grated carrot and simmer for another 2–3 minutes. Adjust the seasoning, discard the bay leaf, and serve sprinkled liberally with chopped fresh parsley.

5 ▲ To make a creamed soup, first blend the leftovers (about half the original soup) in a blender or food processor, or press through a strainer, until smooth, and then return to a clean saucepan with the milk. Bring to a boil and simmer for 2–3 minutes. Adjust the seasoning, and stir in the cream before serving sprinkled with the parsley.

SMOKY HADDOCK SOUP

Smoked haddock gives this soup a good rich flavor, while mashed potatoes and cream thicken and enrich the stock.

SERVES 4–6

INGREDIENTS:
8 ounces smoked haddock
   fillet
1 onion, chopped finely
1 garlic clove, crushed
2¼ cups water
2¼ cups milk
1–1¼ cups hot mashed potatoes
2 tbsp butter
about 1 tbsp lemon juice
6 tbsp heavy cream, sour cream, or
   fromage blanc
4 tbsp chopped fresh parsley
salt and pepper

1 Put the fish, onion, garlic, and water into a saucepan. Bring to a boil, cover, and simmer gently for about 15–20 minutes, until the fish is tender.

2 ▼ Remove the fish from the pan; strip off the skin, and remove all the bones. Flake the flesh finely.

3 Return the skin and bones to the cooking liquid and simmer for 10 minutes. Strain, discarding the skin and bones, and pour the liquid into a clean saucepan.

4 Add the milk, flaked fish, and seasoning to the saucepan. Bring to a boil and simmer for about 3 minutes.

5 ▲ Gradually whisk in enough mashed potato to produce a fairly thick soup, then stir in the butter. Sharpen the soup to taste with a little lemon juice.

6 ▼ Add the cream, sour cream, or fromage blanc, and 3 tablespoons of the parsley. Reheat gently, sprinkle with the remaining parsley, and serve.

VICHYSSOISE

*This is a classic creamy soup made
from potatoes and leeks. To achieve
the delicate pale color, be sure to use
only the white parts of the leeks.
Vichyssoise is also excellent served hot.*

SERVES 4–6

INGREDIENTS:
*3 large leeks
3 tbsp butter or margarine
1 onion, sliced thinly
1 pound potatoes, chopped
3½ cups fresh chicken or vegetable stock
2 tsp lemon juice
pinch of ground nutmeg
¼ tsp ground coriander
1 dried bay leaf
1 egg yolk
¾ cup light cream
salt and white pepper
snipped fresh chives, or crisply fried
    and crumbled bacon, to garnish*

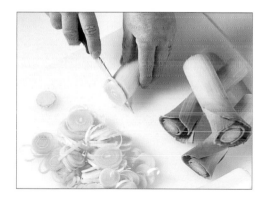

1 ▲ Trim the leeks and remove most
of the green part (it can be served as a
vegetable). Slice the white part of the
leeks very finely.

2 Melt the butter or margarine in a
saucepan, and fry the leeks and onion
gently for about 5 minutes without
browning, stirring from time to time.

3 ▼ Add the potatoes, stock, lemon
juice, seasoning, nutmeg, coriander,
and bay leaf to the pan. Bring to a
boil. Cover and simmer for about
30 minutes, until all the vegetables are
very soft.

4 Cool the soup a little, discard the
bay leaf, and then press the soup
through a strainer, or blend in a food
processor or blender, until smooth.
Pour into a clean saucepan.

5 ▼ Blend the egg yolk into the light
cream, add a little of the soup to the
mixture, and then whisk it all back
into the soup and reheat gently
without boiling. Adjust seasoning
to taste.

6 Leave to cool, and then cover and
chill thoroughly in the refrigerator.
Garnish the soup with snipped chives,
or crisply fried and crumbled bacon,
and serve chilled.

MICROWAVE BEET SOUP

A deep red soup of blended beets and potatoes, this makes a stunning first course. Adding a swirl of sour cream and a few sprigs of dill produces a very pretty effect.

SERVES 4

INGREDIENTS:
1 onion, chopped
3 cups diced potatoes
1 small cooking apple, peeled, cored, and grated
3 tbsp water
1 tsp cumin seeds
2 cups peeled, diced, and cooked red beets
1 dried bay leaf
pinch of dried thyme
1 tsp lemon juice
2½ cups hot vegetable stock
4 tbsp sour cream
salt and pepper
sprigs of fresh dill, to garnish

1 Place the onion, potatoes, apple, and water in a large bowl. Cover and cook on high power for 10 minutes.

2 ▲ Stir in the cumin seeds and cook on high power for 1 minute.

3 ▲ Stir in the beets, bay leaf, thyme, lemon juice, and stock. Cover and cook on high power for 12 minutes, stirring halfway through.

4 Leave to stand, uncovered, for 5 minutes. Remove the bay leaf. Strain the vegetables and reserve the liquid. Blend the vegetables with a little of the reserved liquid in a food processor or blender, until the soup becomes smooth and creamy. Alternatively, mash the ingredients or press the soup through a strainer.

5 Pour the vegetable purée into a clean bowl with the reserved liquid and mix well. Season to taste. Cover and cook on high power for 4–5 minutes until piping hot.

6 ▲ Serve the soup in warmed bowls. Swirl 1 tablespoon of sour cream into each serving and garnish with a few sprigs of fresh dill.

MINTED PEA & YOGURT SOUP

This deliciously refreshing soup is also nutritious. It is extremely tasty when served chilled – in which case you may like to thin the consistency a little more with extra stock, yogurt, or milk, as wished.

SERVES 6

INGREDIENTS:
2 tbsp vegetable oil or ghee
2 onions, peeled and coarsely chopped
2 cups peeled and coarsely chopped
   potatoes
2 garlic cloves, peeled
1-inch piece fresh ginger, peeled and
   chopped
1 tsp ground coriander
1 tsp ground cumin
1 tbsp all-purpose flour
3¼ cups fresh vegetable stock
3 cups frozen peas
2–3 tbsp chopped fresh mint, to taste
salt and pepper
⅔ cup strained thick plain yogurt
½ tsp cornstarch
1¼ cups milk
a little extra yogurt, to serve
   (optional)
sprigs of fresh mint,
   to garnish

1 ▼ Heat the oil or ghee in a saucepan, add the onions and potato, and cook gently for 3 minutes. Stir in the garlic, ginger, coriander, cumin, and flour, and cook for 1 minute, stirring.

3 Reduce the heat, cover, and simmer gently for 15 minutes, or until the vegetables are tender.

4 ▼ Blend the soup, in batches, in a blender or food processor to a purée. Return the mixture to the saucepan and season to taste. Blend the yogurt with the cornstarch and stir into the soup.

5 ▼ Add the milk and bring almost to a boil, stirring all the time. Cook very gently for 2 minutes. Serve hot, with a swirl of extra yogurt, if wished, and garnished with the mint.

2 Add the stock, peas, and half the mint. Bring to a boil, stirring.

INDIAN BEAN SOUP

This soup is substantial enough to serve as a main meal with whole wheat bread. Black-eyed peas are used here, but red kidney beans or garbanzo beans may be added if preferred.

SERVES 4–6

INGREDIENTS:

4 tbsp vegetable oil
 or ghee
2 onions, peeled and chopped
1¼ cups potato, peeled and cut
 into chunks
1¼ cups parsnip, peeled and cut
 into chunks
1¼ cups turnip or rutabaga, peeled and
 cut into chunks
2 celery stalks, trimmed and
 sliced
2 zucchini, trimmed and sliced
1 green bell pepper, cored,
 deseeded, and cut into
 ½-inch pieces
2 garlic cloves, crushed
2 tsp ground coriander
1 tbsp paprika
1 tbsp mild curry paste
5 cups fresh vegetable stock
salt
15-ounce can black-eyed peas, drained
 and rinsed
chopped fresh cilantro, to garnish
 (optional)

1 Heat the oil or ghee in a saucepan, add all the prepared vegetables, except the zucchini and bell pepper, and cook over a medium heat for 5 minutes, stirring frequently. Add the garlic, coriander, paprika, and curry paste, and cook for 1 minute, stirring.

2 ▼ Stir in the stock and season with salt to taste. Bring to a boil, cover, and simmer gently for 25 minutes, stirring occasionally.

3 ▼ Stir in the black-eyed peas, sliced zucchini, and green bell pepper, cover

and continue cooking for 15 minutes more, or until all the vegetables are tender.

4 ▲ Blend 1¼ cups of the soup mixture (about 2 ladlefuls) to a purée in a food processor or blender. Return the mixture to the soup in the saucepan and reheat until piping hot.

5 Sprinkle with chopped cilantro, if using, and serve hot.

MINESTRONE WITH PESTO

This is one of the many versions of minestrone, which always includes vegetables, pasta, and rice, and often beans. This soup is flavored with pesto, so often added to pasta dishes.

SERVES 6

INGREDIENTS:
scant 1 cup dried cannellini beans, soaked overnight
10 cups water or stock
1 large onion, peeled and chopped
1 leek, trimmed and thinly sliced
2 celery stalks, very thinly sliced
2 carrots, peeled and chopped
3 tbsp olive oil
2 tomatoes, skinned and roughly chopped
1 zucchini, trimmed and thinly sliced
2 potatoes, peeled and diced
¾ cup elbow macaroni, or other small macaroni
salt and pepper
4–6 tbsp grated Parmesan

PESTO:
2 tbsp pine nut
5 tbsp olive oil
2 bunches fresh basil, stems removed
4–6 garlic cloves, crushed
¾ cup grated Pecorino or Parmesan cheese
salt and pepper

1 ▼ Drain the beans, rinse, and place in a saucepan with the measured water or stock. Bring to a boil, cover, and simmer gently for 1 hour.

2 ▲ Add the onion, leek, celery, carrots, and oil. Cover and simmer for 4–5 minutes.

3 Add the tomatoes, zucchini, potatoes, macaroni, and seasoning. Cover again and continue to simmer for about 30 minutes, or until very tender.

4 Meanwhile, make the pesto. Fry the pine nuts in 1 tablespoon of the oil until pale brown, then drain.

5 Put the basil into a food processor or blender with the nuts and garlic. Process until well chopped. Gradually add the oil, little by little, until smooth. Transfer the sauce to a bowl, add the cheese and seasoning, and mix thoroughly.

6 ▲ Stir 1½ tablespoons of the pesto into the soup until well blended. Simmer for 5 minutes more and adjust the seasoning. Serve very hot, sprinkled with the cheese.

HUNGARIAN SAUSAGE SOUP

A rich, warming soup, based on the famous Hungarian goulash, which uses beef instead of sausage.

SERVES 4

INGREDIENTS:
2 tbsp olive oil
2 onions, chopped
2 garlic cloves, chopped
1 tbsp paprika
1 pound potatoes, diced
1 red bell pepper, deseeded and diced
14-ounce can chopped tomatoes
1 tbsp tomato paste
1 fresh bay leaf
2 tsp caraway seeds
3¾ cups beef stock
6 ounces kabanos sausage, sliced
2 tbsp chopped fresh parsley
4 tbsp sour cream
salt and pepper
crusty bread, to serve

1 ▼ Heat the oil in a saucepan and fry the onion over a high heat for 2 minutes. Add the garlic and paprika, and fry briefly.

2 ▼ Add the potato, red bell pepper, tomatoes, tomato paste, bay leaf, caraway seeds, stock, and seasoning.

3 Cover and simmer for 10–15 minutes, then add the kabanos sausage and parsley, and cook for 2 minutes more.

4 ▲ Pour the soup into warm bowls and spoon a little of sour cream into each bowl. Serve with crusty bread.

POTATOES IN TOMATO & OLIVE DRESSING

The warm potatoes quickly absorb the wonderful flavors of olives, tomatoes, and olive oil. This salad is delicious when served warm, but it is also good served cold.

SERVES 4

INGREDIENTS:
1½ pounds waxy, round white potatoes
1 shallot
2 tomatoes
1 tbsp chopped fresh basil
salt

TOMATO AND OLIVE DRESSING:
1 tomato, skinned and chopped finely
4 black olives, pitted and chopped finely
4 tbsp olive oil
1 tbsp wine vinegar
1 garlic clove, crushed
salt and pepper

1 Cook the potatoes in boiling, salted water for 15 minutes until tender.

2 ▼ Drain the potatoes well, chop roughly, and put into a bowl. Chop the shallot. Cut the tomatoes into wedges, and add the shallot and tomatoes to the warm potatoes.

3 ▼ To make the dressing, put all the ingredients into a screw-top jar and shake to mix together.

4 ▲ Pour the dressing over the potato mixture and toss well. Transfer the salad to a serving dish and sprinkle with the chopped fresh basil.

MEXICAN SALAD

Cooked new potatoes and blanched cauliflower are combined with carrots, olives, capers, and sweet gherkins in a tangy mustard dressing to make a salad that is suitable as an accompaniment or as a main dish.

SERVES 4

INGREDIENTS:
1 pound small new potatoes, scraped
salt
8 ounces small cauliflower florets
1–2 carrots, peeled
3 large sweet gherkins
2–3 scallions, trimmed
1–2 tbsp capers
12 pitted black olives
1 iceberg lettuce or other lettuce leaves

DRESSING:
1½–2 tsp Dijon mustard
1 tsp sugar
2 tbsp olive oil
4 tbsp mayonnaise
1 tbsp wine vinegar
salt and pepper

TO GARNISH:
1 ripe avocado
1 tbsp lime or lemon juice

1 Cook the potatoes in salted water until they are just tender. Drain, cool, and either dice or slice them. Cook the cauliflower in boiling, salted water for 2 minutes. Drain, rinse in cold water, and drain again.

2 Cut the carrots into narrow julienne strips, and mix with the potatoes and cauliflower.

3 ▼ Cut the sweet gherkins and scallions, slicing on the diagonal, and add them to the vegetable salad, together with the capers and black olives.

4 ▲ Arrange the lettuce leaves on a large serving plate or bowl, or in individual bowls, and spoon the salad over the lettuce.

5 ▲ To make the dressing, whisk all the ingredients together until completely emulsified. Drizzle the dressing over the salad.

6 ▼ Cut the avocado into quarters, then remove the pit, and peel. Cut into slices and dip immediately in the lime or lemon juice. Use to garnish the salad just before serving.

GARDEN SALAD

This chunky salad includes tiny new potatoes tossed in a minty dressing, and has a mustard dip for dunking.

SERVES 6-8

INGREDIENTS:

1 pound tiny new or salad potatoes
4 tbsp French salad dressing, or
* vinaigrette*
2 tbsp chopped fresh mint
8 ounces broccoli florets
4 ounces sugar snap peas or snow peas,
* trimmed*
2 large carrots
4 celery stalks
1 yellow or orange bell pepper, halved,
* cored, and deseeded*
1 bunch scallions, trimmed
* (optional)*
1 head endive

MUSTARD DIP:

6 tbsp sour cream
3 tbsp mayonnaise
2 tsp balsamic vinegar
1½ tsp coarse-grain mustard
¼ tsp creamed horseradish
good pinch of brown sugar
salt and pepper

1 Cook the potatoes in boiling, salted water until just tender – about 10 minutes. While they cook, combine the dressing or vinaigrette and mint.

2 ▼ Drain the potatoes thoroughly, add to the dressing while hot, toss well, and leave until cold, giving an occasional stir.

3 ▼ To make the dip, combine the sour cream, mayonnaise, vinegar, mustard, horseradish, sugar, and seasoning. Transfer to a serving bowl, cover, and refrigerate until ready to serve.

4 Cut the broccoli into bite-size florets and blanch for 2 minutes in boiling water. Drain and toss immediately in cold water; when cold, drain thoroughly.

5 Blanch the sugar snap peas or snow peas in the same way, but only for 1 minute. Drain, rinse in cold water, and drain again.

6 Cut the carrots and celery into sticks measuring about 2½ × ½ inches. Slice the bell pepper or cut into cubes. Cut off some of the green part of the scallions, if using, and separate the endive leaves.

7 ▲ Arrange the vegetables attractively in a fairly shallow bowl with the potatoes piled up in the center. Serve accompanied with the mustard dip.

POTATO & SMOKED HAM MAYONNAISE

This delicious mixture of potato, egg, and smoked ham, mixed with a mustard mayonnaise, is ideal for a light lunch. You can use sliced frankfurters cut into cubes instead of the smoked ham, if you prefer.

SERVES 4

INGREDIENTS:
1½ pounds new potatoes, scrubbed
4 scallions, chopped
2 tbsp French dressing or vinaigrette
⅔ cup mayonnaise
3 tbsp thick plain yogurt
1 tbsp Dijon mustard
2 eggs
8-ounce slice of smoked ham
3 sweet gherkins
2 tbsp chopped fresh dill

1 Cook the potatoes in boiling, salted water for 15 minutes, until just tender, then drain.

2 ▼ Cut the potatoes into pieces and put into a bowl, while still warm, with the scallion and dressing. Mix together well.

3 Mix the mayonnaise, yogurt, and mustard together. Set aside.

4 Boil the eggs for 12 minutes, then plunge into cold water to cool. Shell and chop roughly.

5 ▼ Cut the smoked ham into cubes and slice the gherkins.

6 ▲ Add the cubed ham and sliced gherkins to the potatoes with the chopped egg. Pour over the mayonnaise and mustard mixture, and mix the salad together carefully to combine.

7 Transfer the potato salad to a large serving dish, sprinkle with the chopped fresh dill, and serve.

THREE-WAY POTATO SALAD

There's nothing to beat the flavor of new potatoes, served warm in a delicious dressing.

EACH DRESSING SERVES 4

INGREDIENTS:
1 pound new potatoes for each dressing
fresh herbs, to garnish

LIGHT CURRY DRESSING:
1 tbsp vegetable oil
1 tbsp medium curry paste
1 small onion, chopped
1 tbsp mango chutney, chopped
6 tbsp plain yogurt
3 tbsp light cream
2 tbsp mayonnaise
salt and pepper
1 tbsp light cream, to garnish

WARM VINAIGRETTE DRESSING:
6 tbsp hazelnut oil
3 tbsp cider vinegar
1 tsp coarse-grain mustard
1 tsp superfine sugar
few fresh basil leaves, torn into shreds
salt and pepper

PARSLEY, SCALLION, & SOUR CREAM DRESSING:
⅔ cup sour cream
3 tbsp light mayonnaise
4 scallions, trimmed and chopped finely
1 tbsp chopped fresh parsley
salt and pepper

1 To make the Light Curry Dressing, heat the vegetable oil in a saucepan, and then add the curry paste and onion. Fry together, stirring frequently, for about 5 minutes, until the onion is soft. Remove from the heat and let cool slightly.

2 ▼ Mix together the mango chutney, yogurt, cream, and mayonnaise. Add the curry mixture and blend together. Season with salt and pepper.

3 ▼ To make the Warm Vinaigrette Dressing, whisk the hazelnut oil, cider vinegar, mustard, sugar, and basil together in a small pitcher or bowl. Season with salt and pepper.

4 ▲ To make the Parsley, Scallion, & Sour Cream Dressing, mix all the ingredients together until completely combined. Season with salt and pepper.

5 Cook the potatoes in lightly salted, boiling water until just tender. Drain well and let cool for 5 minutes, then add the chosen dressing, tossing to coat. Garnish with fresh herbs, and spoon a little light cream on to the potatoes if you have used the curry dressing, and serve.

HOT POTATO & HAM SALAD

This is a very adaptable salad. With potatoes as a base, you can vary the additional ingredients, using egg, pickled herring, or red beets instead of the smoked ham. It is excellent served as a light lunch.

SERVES 4

INGREDIENTS:

6 ounces smoked ham
1 pound salad potatoes
6 scallions, white and green
 parts sliced
3 sweet gherkins, sliced
4 tbsp mayonnaise
4 tbsp thick plain yogurt
2 tbsp chopped fresh dill
salt

1 ▼ Cut the ham into 1½-inch long strips.

2 ▼ Cut the potatoes into ½-inch cubes and cook in boiling, salted water for 8 minutes, until tender.

3 ▲ Drain the potatoes and return to the saucepan with the scallions, ham, and cucumber.

4 ▼ Mix in the mayonnaise, yogurt, and dill, and stir to coat the potatoes. Transfer to a warmed dish and serve.

BASIL, POTATO, & PIMIENTO SALAD

Bags of mixed salad leaves, available from supermarkets, can be used instead of the lettuces in this robust and colorful salad. The vinaigrette is added to warm potatoes, so they absorb some of the flavor.

SERVES 4

INGREDIENTS:
1½ pound new potatoes, scrubbed
½ tsp salt
1 oak leaf lettuce
½ romaine lettuce
watercress or arugula leaves
1 small red onion, sliced finely
4 ounces canned red pimiento, drained
12 pitted black olives
handful of fresh basil leaves
salt and pepper

VINAIGRETTE:
6 tbsp olive oil
3 tbsp red wine vinegar
1 tsp Dijon mustard
pinch of superfine sugar
salt and pepper

1 ▼ Put the potatoes into a saucepan of cold water. Bring to a boil, add the salt, then cover and simmer for about 20 minutes, until tender.

2 ▼ Meanwhile make the vinaigrette by whisking the olive oil, vinegar, mustard, sugar, and seasoning together in a small bowl.

3 Drain the potatoes, cut into quarters, and place in a large bowl. Pour over the vinaigrette and let cool.

4 Arrange the lettuce leaves, watercress or arugula, and

onion on 4 serving plates. Pile one-quarter of the dressed potatoes on each salad. Alternatively, arrange the ingredients on a large serving platter.

5 ▲ Slice the pimientos into narrow strips and arrange over the potatoes. Place 3 olives on each serving. Tear the basil leaves into shreds and sprinkle over the salads. Season with extra salt and pepper, and serve.

LAYERED CHICKEN SALAD

This layered main-course salad has lively tastes and textures. For an interesting variation, substitute canned tuna for the chicken. You can also use a commercial brand of vinaigrette or Caesar salad dressing, instead of this homemade dressing.

SERVES 4

INGREDIENTS:
1½ pounds new potatoes, scrubbed
1 red bell pepper, halved, cored, and
   deseeded
1 green bell pepper, halved, cored, and
   deseeded
2 small zucchini, sliced
1 small onion, thinly sliced
3 tomatoes, sliced
12 ounces cooked chicken, sliced
snipped fresh chives, to garnish

YOGURT DRESSING:
⅔ cup plain yogurt
3 tbsp mayonnaise
1 tbsp snipped fresh chives
salt and pepper

1 Put the potatoes into a large saucepan of cold water. Bring to a boil, then reduce the heat. Cover and simmer for 15–20 minutes, until tender.

2 Meanwhile place the bell pepper halves, cut side down, under a preheated hot broiler and broil until the skins blacken and begin to char. Remove and cover with a clean, damp cloth. Leave to cool, then peel off the skins and slice the flesh. Set aside.

3 ▼ Cook the sliced zucchini in a small amount of lightly salted, boiling water for 3 minutes. Rinse with cold water to cool quickly and set aside.

4 ▼ Make the dressing. Mix the yogurt, mayonnaise, and snipped chives together in a small bowl. Season well with salt and pepper.

5 ▲ Drain, cool, and slice the potatoes. Add them to the dressing and mix well to coat evenly. Divide between 4 serving plates. Top each plate with one-quarter of the bell pepper slices and cooked zucchini. Layer one-quarter of the onion and tomato slices, then the sliced chicken, on top of each serving. Garnish with snipped chives and serve.

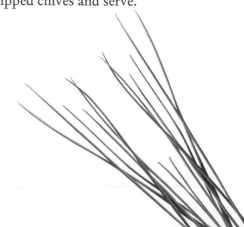

BACON & EGG SALAD WITH CRISPY FRIED POTATOES

Crispy bacon bits, hard-cooked egg, and cubes of crispy fried potato make a very tasty salad on a bed of lettuce. Four regular eggs can be substituted for the quail's eggs.

SERVES 4

INGREDIENTS:

8 ounces potatoes, scrubbed
½ tsp salt
3 tbsp olive oil
1 tbsp butter
4 ounces smoked bacon
8–12 quail's eggs,
  hard-cooked
1 large bag mixed lettuce leaves

LEMON DRESSING:

3 tbsp olive oil
1 tsp finely grated lemon rind
1½ tbsp lemon juice
1 tbsp chopped fresh parsley
  or cilantro
salt and pepper

1 Put the potatoes into a large saucepan of cold water. Bring to a boil, add the salt, and then reduce the heat. Cover and simmer for 15 minutes, until just tender. Drain, let cool, peel, and dice.

2 ▼ Heat the olive oil and butter in a large skillet. Add the diced potatoes and gently fry over a medium–high heat for 8–10 minutes, until browned and crisp. When crispy, remove with a perforated spoon and drain on paper towels.

3 ▼ Meanwhile broil the bacon under a preheated hot broiler until very crisp. Drain on paper towels and snip into tiny pieces. Cut each of the cooked quail's eggs in half.

4 Rinse the lettuce and arrange on 4 plates. Scatter one-quarter of the potatoes over each salad. Divide the eggs between the plates, and sprinkle each salad with crispy bacon bits.

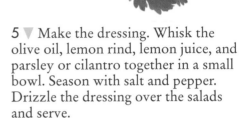

5 ▼ Make the dressing. Whisk the olive oil, lemon rind, lemon juice, and parsley or cilantro together in a small bowl. Season with salt and pepper. Drizzle the dressing over the salads and serve.

RUSSIAN SALAD

This classic salad is perfect for the winter months, because it makes the most of a selection of root vegetables. For a lighter dressing, substitute a low-fat mayonnaise, or else mix equal quantities of low-fat plain yogurt with regular mayonnaise.

SERVES 4

INGREDIENTS:
3 medium potatoes, peeled and
    quartered
½ tsp salt
1 carrot
1 turnip
½ small cauliflower, broken into
    tiny florets
½ cup frozen peas, thawed
2 tomatoes, skinned, deseeded,
    and diced
½ cup cooked, peeled shrimp
½ cup diced, cooked ham

CAPER DRESSING:
4 sweet gherkins, chopped
1 tbsp capers
4–5 tbsp mayonnaise
salt and pepper

TO SERVE:
¼ iceberg lettuce,
    shredded
1 cooked beet, diced
sweet gherkins
stuffed green olives, sliced
sprigs of fresh parsley

1 Put the potatoes into a large saucepan of cold water. Bring to a boil, add the salt, then reduce the heat. Cover and simmer for 15–20 minutes, until tender. Drain, cool slightly, and dice. Set aside.

2 ▼ While the potatoes are cooking, dice the carrot and turnip, and cook with the cauliflower in lightly salted, boiling water for 5–8 minutes until tender. Drain and leave to cool.

3 ▼ In a large bowl, mix together the potatoes, carrot, turnip, cauliflower, thawed peas, and tomatoes. Add the

shrimp and diced ham, and stir well to combine.

4 ▼ Make the dressing. Combine the gherkins and capers with the mayonnaise in a small bowl. Season with salt and pepper. Add to the salad and stir well to coat evenly.

5 Arrange the lettuce on 4 serving plates. Pile one-quarter of the salad mixture on each plate. Arrange little mounds of beet at the side of each salad. Using a sharp knife, make several lengthwise cuts in each gherkin, leaving one end intact and then fanning out the gherkin. Garnish the salads with the gherkin fans, sliced olives, and parsley.

SNACKS & LIGHT MEALS

This chapter celebrates the versatility of potatoes, showing you how to create a fabulous array of hors d'eouvres and party nibbles, as well as quick and healthy lunches or snacks. Along with such favorites as potato skins with dips and filled baked potatoes, which are suitable for family lunches and for children, there are more elegant dishes, such as Crab & Potato Balls and Almond Potato Bites, that would be ideal to serve as appetizers for more sophisticated dinner parties. A wide selection of potato fritters and cakes is also featured, from spicy and exotically flavored recipes to milder cheese and herb varieties. There are samosas, pasties, and other little deep-fried pastries that are filled with a blend of ingredients; some of which are vegetarian, while others include meat. For those who like the combination of eggs and potatoes, there are several omelet dishes, such as the frittata-style Spanish Omelet and the colorful Flamenco Eggs. There are also Picnic Omelet Squares, which are delicious served cold, like tapas.

DEVILED NEW POTATOES

This is a way of giving potatoes, or any other root vegetable you have to hand, the star treatment. A barbecue needs smaller things like this to keep your diners happy while they wait for the main event. You will need to soak the wooden toothpicks in hand-hot water for 20 minutes before using.

SERVES 6–8

INGREDIENTS:
20 wooden toothpicks
1 pound baby new potatoes
olive oil for brushing
10 slices bacon
20 small sage leaves

1 ▼ Bring a pan of water to a boil and add the potatoes. Boil for 10 minutes, then drain.

2 ▼ Brush the potatoes all over with olive oil.

3 ▼ Cut each bacon slice in half widthwise. Holding each piece at one end, smooth and stretch it with the back of a knife.

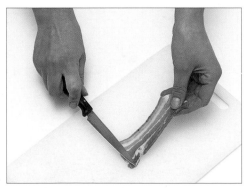

4 ▲ Wrap a piece of bacon around each new potato, enclosing a sage leaf and securing with a wooden toothpick.

5 Cook over a prepared hot grill, or under a preheated hot broiler, for 6–7 minutes, turning occasionally. Serve hot or cold.

CRAB & POTATO BALLS

These make an unusual first course. They are very popular in the Dominican Republic, where they may also be made with chopped shrimp. Serve them with a rich tomato sauce, if you like.

MAKES 30

INGREDIENTS:
1 pound potatoes, cut into chunks
3 tbsp butter
2 egg yolks
⅓ cup grated Edam cheese
1 tbsp finely chopped fresh flat-leaf
  parsley
1 onion, finely chopped
2 cups crabmeat
all-purpose flour, for coating
1 egg, beaten
⅓ cup dry white bread crumbs
vegetable oil, for deep-frying
salt and pepper

TO GARNISH:
lemon or lime wedges
spinach leaves

1 ▼ Cook the potatoes in boiling, salted water until tender. Drain and mash with 2 tablespoons of the butter, the egg yolks, cheese, parsley, and seasoning. Set aside.

2 Heat the remaining butter in a small skillet and sauté the onion until soft, but not brown.

3 Transfer the onion to a bowl and let cool.

4 ▼ Add the crabmeat and mashed potato to the onion and combine well. Form into 30 small equal-size balls. Place on a baking sheet lined with parchment paper and refrigerate for at least 30 minutes.

5 Put the flour and bread crumbs in separate shallow dishes or on plates. Roll the balls in the flour, dip them in the beaten egg, and then coat evenly with the bread crumbs.

6 ▼ Half-fill a deep-fat fryer or saucepan with oil and heat to 375°F, or until a cube of bread browns in 40 seconds. Deep-fry the balls in batches for 5–6 minutes, until golden brown all over. Remove with a perforated spoon and drain on paper towels. Keep warm until all the balls have been cooked.

7 Serve garnished with lemon or lime wedges and spinach leaves.

PAKORAS

These vegetable fritters are easy to make and good to eat. They may be served as a tasty appetizer, or as an accompaniment to a main course.

SERVES 4–6

❋❋❋❋❋❋❋❋❋❋❋❋❋❋❋❋

INGREDIENTS:
4 ounces broccoli
1 onion
2 potatoes
1½ cups gram flour
1 tsp garam masala
1½ tsp salt
¼ tsp chili powder
1 tsp cumin seeds
just under 1 cup water
vegetable oil, for deep-frying
sprigs of cilantro, to garnish

❋❋❋❋❋❋❋❋❋❋❋❋❋❋❋❋

1 ▼ Cut the broccoli into small florets, discarding most of the stalk, and cook in a pan of boiling, salted water for 4 minutes. Drain well, return to the pan, and shake dry over a low heat for a few minutes. Place the broccoli on paper towels to let them dry completely while preparing the other vegetables.

2 Peel and thinly slice the onion, and separate it into rings. Peel and thinly slice the potatoes, and pat them dry.

3 ▼ Place the gram flour in a bowl with the garam masala, salt, chili powder, and cumin seeds. Make a well in the center, add the water, and mix to form a smooth batter. Dip the vegetables into the batter to coat them completely.

4 ▲ Fill a deep-fat fryer or saucepan one-third full with oil and heat to 375°F, or until a cube of bread browns in 30 seconds. Lower the vegetables into the hot oil and fry, in batches, for 3–4 minutes, or until golden brown and crisp. Drain the vegetables on paper towels and keep them warm while cooking the rest in the same way. Serve the pakoras hot, garnished with cilantro.

SAMOSAS WITH SPICY DIP

A spicy filling of ground meat and vegetables is enclosed in a pastry crescent, and is excellent served with a spicy dip. If you are packing the samosas for a picnic, or in a lunch-box, fry the samosas 2–3 hours ahead of time.

MAKES 16

INGREDIENTS:
1 onion, finely chopped
1 garlic clove, crushed
1 tsp freshly grated fresh ginger
2 tbsp oil
1 carrot, grated coarsely
1½ tsp garam masala
½ cup cooked ground beef, pork, or ham
¾ cup cooked peas
1 cup cooked potatoes, diced finely
salt and pepper

PASTRY:
2 cups all-purpose flour
½ tsp salt
2 tbsp butter or margarine
scant ½ cup cold water
vegetable oil, for deep-frying

SPICY DIP:
½ cup mayonnaise
3 tbsp sour cream or fromage blanc
1½ tsp curry powder
½ tsp ground coriander
1 tsp tomato paste
2 tbsp mango chutney, chopped
1 tbsp chopped fresh parsley

1 To make the filling, fry the onion, garlic, and ginger in the oil until soft. Add the carrot and fry for 2–3 minutes. Stir in the garam masala and 4 tablespoons water, season, and simmer gently until almost all the liquid is absorbed. Remove the pan from the heat, stir in the meat, peas, and potatoes, and leave the mixture to cool.

2 To make the pastry, sift the flour and salt into a bowl, then cut in the butter. Add enough of the water to mix to a smooth, elastic dough, kneading continually. Cut the dough into 16 pieces and keep covered. Dip each piece into a little oil, or coat lightly with flour, and roll out to a 5-inch circle.

3 ▼ Put 1–2 tablespoons of the filling on one side of each pastry circle, dampen the edge, fold over, and seal firmly. Keep the samosas covered with a damp cloth.

4 ▼ In a deep-fat fryer or saucepan, heat the oil to 350–375°F, or until a cube of bread browns in about 30 seconds. Fry the samosas a few at a time for 3–4 minutes, until golden brown, turning once or twice. Drain on paper towels.

5 To make the dip, combine all the ingredients in a separate bowl. Serve the samosas hot or cold with the dip.

VEGETABLE & CASHEW SAMOSAS

These nutty little fried pastries are really quite simple to make. Serve them hot as an appetizer to an Indian meal, or cold as a tasty picnic or lunch-box snack.

MAKES 12

INGREDIENTS:
*3 cups peeled and diced potatoes
salt
1 cup frozen peas
3 tbsp vegetable oil
1 onion, peeled and chopped
1-inch piece fresh ginger, peeled and
    chopped
1 garlic clove, peeled and crushed
1 tsp garam masala
2 tsp mild curry paste
⅓ tsp cumin seeds
2 tsp lemon juice
⅓ cup unsalted cashews, coarsely
    chopped
vegetable oil, for shallow frying
sprigs of cilantro, to garnish
mango chutney, to serve*

PASTRY:
*2 cups all-purpose flour
⅓ cup butter
⅓ cup warm milk*

out to within ⅓ inch of the edges. Brush the edges of pastry all the way around with water and fold over to form triangular shapes, sealing the edges well together to enclose the filling completely.

1 Cook the potatoes in a saucepan of boiling, salted water for 5 minutes. Add the peas and cook for 4 minutes more, or until the potato is tender. Drain well. Heat the oil in a skillet, add the onion, potato, and pea mixture, the ginger, garlic, and spices, and fry for 2 minutes. Stir in the lemon juice and cook gently, uncovered, for 2 minutes. Remove from the heat, slightly mash the potato and peas, then add the cashews. Mix well and season with salt.

2 ▲ To make the pastry, put the flour in a bowl and cut in the butter. Mix in the milk to form a dough. Knead lightly and divide into 6 balls. Roll out each ball on a lightly floured surface to an 7-inch round. Cut each round in half.

3 ▼ Divide the filling equally between each semicircle of pastry, spreading it

4 ▲ Fill a large deep-fat fryer or saucepan one-third full with oil and heat to 350°F, or until a cube of bread browns in 30 seconds. Fry the samosas, a few at a time, turning frequently until golden brown and heated through. Drain on paper towels and keep warm while cooking the rest in the same way. Garnish with cilantro sprigs and serve hot.

TUNA & VEGETARIAN PARCELS

I first encountered this recipe in a Fijian–Indian restaurant in Sydney. In order to quench our hunger as we waited for our food, we were served these memorable tuna parcels. Each filling recipe makes enough to fill all the pastry.

MAKES 32

INGREDIENTS:
PASTRY:
4 cups all-purpose flour
¼ tsp turmeric
¼ tsp salt
*scant ¼ cup ghee or
    clarified butter*
*scant 1 cup milk, mixed with a
    little lemon juice*

TUNA FILLING:
¼ tsp ground turmeric
¼ tsp chili powder
1 tsp ground cumin
1 tsp ground coriander
7-ounce can tuna, drained
¼ cup frozen peas, cooked
¼ cup diced boiled potatoes
salt and pepper

VEGETARIAN FILLING:
8 ounces white potatoes, boiled
*14-ounce can artichoke hearts,
    drained and blended to a
    purée*
1 tsp black pepper, ground
2 tsp coriander seeds, ground
1 tsp cumin seeds, ground
¼ tsp fenugreek seeds, ground
*2 large tomatoes, skinned, deseeded,
    and chopped*
¼ cup frozen peas, cooked

SAUCE:
6 anchovies
2 tbsp plain yogurt

1 To make the pastry, sift the flour, turmeric, and salt into a bowl. Cut in the ghee or butter. Add enough milk to form a fairly soft dough. Cover and set aside.

2 To make the tuna filling, roast the spices in a large skillet. Remove from the heat and add the tuna, peas, and potatoes. Stir well and season. Use to fill the pastry.

3 ▼ To make the vegetarian filling, mash the potatoes and combine with the artichokes. Roast the spices in a large skillet. Remove from the heat and add the potato mixture. Stir well to combine. Carefully fold in the tomatoes and peas. Season and use to fill the pastry.

4 ▼ Roll out the pastry and cut out 5-inch circles. Cut each circle in half, and put a teaspoonful of the tuna or vegetarian filling on each half.

5 Brush the edges with milk and fold each half over to form a triangle. Seal well, and crimp the edges. Bake in a preheated oven at 375°F.

6 To make the sauce, mash the anchovies. Mix the anchovies with the yogurt and season well. Serve with the hot parcels.

POTATO SKINS WITH GUACAMOLE DIP

Although avocados do contain fat, if they are used in small quantities with the right balance of ingredients, you can still enjoy their creamy texture.

SERVES 4

INGREDIENTS:
8 ounces baking potatoes
2 tsp olive oil
coarse sea salt and pepper
snipped fresh chives, to garnish

GUACAMOLE DIP:
6 ounces ripe avocado
1 tbsp lemon juice
2 ripe, firm tomatoes, chopped
  finely
1 tsp grated lemon rind
⅓ cup medium-fat soft cheese with
  herbs and garlic
4 scallions, chopped finely
few drops of Tabasco sauce
salt and pepper

1 Bake the potatoes directly on the oven shelf in a preheated oven at 400°F for 1¼ hours, until tender. Remove the baked potatoes from the oven and let the potatoes cool for 30 minutes. Reset the oven temperature to 425°F.

2 ▼ Halve the potatoes lengthwise and scoop out 2 tablespoons of the flesh from the middle of each potato. Slice each in half again. Place the potato skins on a baking sheet and brush the flesh side lightly with oil. Sprinkle with salt and pepper.

3 Bake for 25 minutes more, until the potato skins are golden and crisp.

4 ▲ Meanwhile, make the guacamole dip. Halve the avocado and discard the pit. Peel off the skin and mash the avocado flesh with the lemon juice in a small bowl.

5 ▼ Transfer to a large bowl and mix with the remaining ingredients. Cover and refrigerate until required.

6 Drain the potato skins on paper towels and transfer them to a warmed serving platter. Garnish with chives. Serve hot with the guacamole dip.

FILLED BAKED POTATOES

Cook these potatoes conventionally, then wrap them in foil and keep them warm at the edge of a grill, if wished, ready to fill with a choice of three inspired mixtures.

EACH DRESSING SERVES 4

INGREDIENTS:
*4 large or 8 medium baking
  potatoes
paprika or chili powder, or chopped
  fresh herbs, to garnish*

MEXICAN CORN RELISH:
*8-ounce can corn kernels, drained
¼ red bell pepper, cored, deseeded, and
  chopped finely
2-inch piece cucumber,
  chopped finely
¼ tsp chili powder
salt and pepper*

BLUE CHEESE FILLING:
*¼ cup full-fat cream cheese
¼ cup fromage blanc
4 ounces Danish blue cheese,
  cut into cubes
1 celery stalk, chopped finely
2 tsp snipped fresh chives
celery salt and pepper*

MUSHROOMS IN SPICY
TOMATO SAUCE:
*2 tbsp butter or margarine
8 ounces mushrooms
¼ cup plain yogurt
1 tbsp tomato paste
2 tsp mild curry powder
salt and pepper*

1 Scrub the potatoes and prick them with a fork. Bake in a preheated oven at 400°F for about 1 hour, until just tender.

2 To make the Mexican Corn Relish, put half the corn kernels into a bowl. Put the rest into a blender or food processor and process for 10–15 seconds, or chop and mash them roughly by hand. Add the puréed corn to the corn kernels with the bell pepper, cucumber, and chili powder. Season to taste. Cover and refrigerate until required.

3 ▼ To make the Blue Cheese Filling, mix the cream cheese and fromage blanc together until smooth in a large mixing bowl. Add the blue cheese, celery, and chives. Season with pepper and celery salt. Cover and refrigerate until required.

4 ▼ To make the Mushrooms in Spicy Tomato Sauce, melt the butter in a small skillet. Add the mushrooms and cook gently for 3–4 minutes. Remove from the heat, and stir in the yogurt, tomato paste, and curry powder. Season to taste.

5 Wrap the cooked potatoes in foil and keep warm at the edge of the grill. Serve the fillings sprinkled with paprika, chili powder, or herbs.

BAKED POTATOES WITH BEANS

Baked potatoes, topped with a tasty mixture of beans in a spicy sauce, provide a deliciously filling, high-fiber dish.

SERVES 6

INGREDIENTS:
6 large baking potatoes
4 tbsp vegetable oil or ghee
1 large onion, chopped
2 garlic cloves, crushed
1 tsp ground turmeric
1 tbsp cumin seeds
2 tbsp mild or medium curry paste
12 ounces cherry tomatoes
14-ounce can black-eyed peas, drained
    and rinsed
14-ounce can red kidney beans,
    drained and rinsed
1 tbsp lemon juice
2 tbsp tomato paste
⅔ cup water
2 tbsp chopped fresh mint
    or cilantro
salt and pepper
sprigs of fresh mint or cilantro,
    to garnish
plain yogurt, to serve

1 ▼ Wash and scrub the potatoes, and prick each one several times with a fork. Place in a preheated oven at 400°F for 1–1¼ hours, or until the potatoes feel soft when gently squeezed.

2 ▼ About 20 minutes before the end of the cooking time, prepare the topping. Heat the ghee or oil in a saucepan, add the onion, and cook gently for 5 minutes, stirring frequently. Add the garlic, turmeric, cumin seeds, and curry paste, and cook gently for 1 minute.

3 Stir in the tomatoes, black-eyed peas and red kidney beans, lemon juice, tomato paste, water, and chopped

mint or cilantro. Season with salt and pepper, then cover and cook gently for about 10 minutes, stirring frequently.

4 ▼ When the potatoes are cooked, cut them in half and mash the flesh lightly with a fork. Spoon the prepared bean mixture on top, garnish with fresh mint or cilantro sprigs, and serve with the plain yogurt.

SPICY FISH & POTATO CAKES

You need nice, floury-textured main-crop potatoes for making these tasty fish cakes. Any white fish of your choice may be used.

SERVES 4

INGREDIENTS:

*1 pound potatoes, peeled and cut into
    even-size pieces
1 pound white fish fillets, such as cod
    or haddock, skinned and boned
6 scallions, sliced
1 fresh green chili, deseeded
2 garlic cloves, peeled
1 tsp salt
1 tbsp medium or hot curry paste
2 eggs, beaten
2¼ cups fresh white bread crumbs
vegetable oil, for
    shallow frying
mango chutney, to serve*

TO GARNISH:
*lime wedges
sprigs of fresh cilantro*

1 ▼ Cook the potatoes in a saucepan of boiling, salted water until tender. Drain well, return the potatoes to the saucepan, and place over a moderate heat for a few moments to dry the potatoes off.

2 Let the potatoes cool slightly, then place in a food processor with the fish, onions, chili, garlic, salt, and curry paste. Process until the ingredients are very finely chopped and blended.

3 ▼ Turn the potato mixture into a bowl, and mix in 2 tablespoons of beaten egg and 1 cup of bread crumbs. Place the remaining beaten egg and bread crumbs in separate dishes.

4 Divide the fish mixture into 8 and, using a spoon to help you (the mixture is quite soft), dip first in the egg, and then coat in the bread crumbs. Carefully shape the mixture into ovals.

5 ▼ Heat enough vegetable oil in a large skillet for shallow frying, and fry the fish cakes over a moderate heat for 3–4 minutes, turning frequently, until they are golden brown and cooked through.

6 Drain on paper towels, and garnish with lime wedges and cilantro sprigs. Serve the fish cakes immediately, accompanied by the mango chutney.

FRITTERS WITH TOMATO RELISH

These are incredibly simple to make and sure to be popular when served as a tempting snack.

MAKES 8

✷✤✷✤✷✤✷✤✷✤✷✤✷✤✷✤✷✤✷✤✷✤✷✤

INGREDIENTS:
¼ *cup whole wheat flour*
¼ *tsp ground coriander*
¼ *tsp cumin seeds*
¼ *tsp chili powder*
¼ *tsp ground turmeric*
¼ *tsp salt*
1 *egg*
3 *tbsp milk*
12 *ounces potatoes, peeled*
1–2 *garlic cloves, crushed*
4 *scallions, trimmed and*
  chopped
¼ *cup canned corn kernels*
vegetable oil, for
  shallow frying

TOMATO RELISH:
1 *onion, peeled*
8 *ounces tomatoes*
2 *tbsp chopped fresh cilantro*
2 *tbsp chopped fresh mint*
2 *tbsp lemon juice*
¼ *tsp roasted cumin seeds*
¼ *tsp salt*
few pinches of chili powder,
  to taste

✷✤✷✤✷✤✷✤✷✤✷✤✷✤✷✤✷✤✷✤✷✤✷✤

1 ▼ First make the relish. Cut the onion and tomatoes into small dice and place in a bowl with the remaining ingredients. Mix together well and leave for at least 15 minutes before serving, to allow the flavors to blend.

2 ▲ Place the flour in a bowl, stir in the coriander, cumin, chili powder, turmeric, and salt, and make a well in the center. Add the egg and milk, and mix in gradually to form a fairly thick batter.

3 Coarsely grate the potatoes, place in a strainer, and rinse well under cold running water. Drain and squeeze dry, then stir into the batter with the garlic, scallions and corn.

4 ▲ Heat about ¼ inch of oil in a large skillet and add a few tablespoonfuls of the mixture at a time, flattening each one to form a thin cake. Fry gently for 2–3 minutes, or until golden brown and cooked through, turning frequently.

5 Drain on paper towels and keep hot while frying the remaining mixture in the same way. Serve hot with the tomato relish.

CORN FRITTERS

An ideal supper dish for two, or for one if you halve the quantities. You can use the remaining corn in another recipe.

SERVES 2

INGREDIENTS:
2 tbsp oil
1 small onion, sliced thinly
1 garlic clove, crushed
12 ounces potatoes
7-ounce can corn kernels, drained
½ tsp dried oregano
1 egg, beaten
*½ cup grated Edam or Gouda
   cheese*
salt and pepper
2–4 eggs
2–4 tomatoes, sliced
sprigs of fresh parsley, to garnish

1 Heat 1 tablespoon of the oil in a nonstick skillet. Add the onion and garlic, and fry very gently until soft, but only lightly colored, stirring frequently. Remove from the heat.

2 ▲ Grate the potatoes coarsely into a bowl, and mix in the corn kernels, oregano, beaten egg, and seasoning. Add the fried onion.

3 ▼ Heat the remaining oil in the skillet. Divide the potato mixture in half and add to the pan to make 2 oval-shaped fritters, leveling and shaping the fritters with a metal spatula.

4 Cook gently for about 10 minutes, until browned underneath and almost cooked through, keeping in shape with the metal spatula and loosening the fritters so they don't stick.

5 ▼ Sprinkle each fritter with the grated cheese and place under a preheated moderately hot broiler until golden brown.

6 Meanwhile, poach either 1 or 2 eggs for each person until just cooked. Transfer the fritters to warmed plates and top each one with the eggs and sliced tomatoes. Garnish with the fresh parsley, and serve at once while still hot.

GOLDEN CHEESE & LEEK POTATO CAKES

Make these tasty potato cakes for a quick and simple supper dish. Serve them with scrambled eggs, if you are very hungry.

SERVES 4

INGREDIENTS:
2 pounds potatoes
4 tbsp milk
¼ cup butter or margarine
2 leeks, chopped finely
1 onion, chopped finely
1½ cups grated Caerphilly or
   cheddar cheese
1 tbsp chopped fresh parsley or chives
1 egg, beaten
2 tbsp water
1½ cups fresh white or brown
   bread crumbs
vegetable oil, for shallow frying
salt and pepper
sprigs of flat-leaf parsley, to garnish
mixed salad, to serve

1 ▼ Cook the potatoes in lightly salted, boiling water until tender. Drain and mash them with the milk and the butter or margarine.

2 Cook the leeks and onion in a small amount of salted, boiling water for about 10 minutes, until tender. Drain.

3 ▼ In a large mixing bowl, combine the leeks and onion with the mashed potato, cheese, and parsley or chives. Season to taste.

4 Beat together the egg and water in a shallow bowl. Sprinkle the bread crumbs into a separate shallow bowl. Shape the potato mixture into 12 even-size cakes, brushing each with the egg mixture, then coating with the bread crumbs.

5 ▲ Heat the oil in a large skillet and fry the potato cakes gently for about 2–3 minutes on each side, until lightly golden. Garnish with parsley and serve with a salad.

ROSTI POTATO CAKE WITH ZUCCHINI & CARROTS

A mixture of coarsely grated potatoes, zucchini, and carrots with fried sliced onions is cooked into a cake in a large skillet and topped with cheese, then finished off under a hot broiler. Serve warm or cold, cut into wedges.

SERVES 6

INGREDIENTS:
2 tbsp vegetable oil
1 large onion, sliced thinly
1 garlic clove, crushed (optional)
2 pounds potatoes
6 ounces zucchini, trimmed
4 ounces carrots
¼ tsp ground coriander
¼ cup sharp Gouda or cheddar cheese, grated (optional)
salt and pepper

1 Heat 1 tablespoon of the oil in a large skillet, add the onion and garlic, if using, and fry gently for about 5 minutes, until soft but only barely colored.

2 ▼ Grate the potatoes coarsely into a bowl. Grate the zucchini and carrots, and mix into the potatoes with the coriander and seasoning until evenly combined, then add the fried onions.

3 ▼ Heat the remaining oil in the skillet, add the potato mixture and cook gently, stirring occasionally, for about 5 minutes. Flatten down into a large cake and cook gently for 6–8 minutes, until the cake is browned underneath and almost cooked through.

4 ▼ Sprinkle the top of the potato cake with the grated cheese, if using, and place under a preheated moderately hot broiler for about 5 minutes, or until lightly browned and cooked through.

5 Loosen the potato cake with a large metal spatula and slip it carefully onto a plate. Leave until cold, then cover with plastic wrap or foil, and chill in the refrigerator until required. Cut into wedges to serve.

FISH CAKES WITH SPICY SAUCE

A smoky flavor gives these fish cakes a special tang, making them very popular with children and adults alike. The spicy sauce is a good way to liven up bottled ketchup.

SERVES 4

INGREDIENTS:
2 pounds potatoes, cut into chunks
¾–1 pound smoked haddock or cod fillet, skinned
1 bay leaf
2 hard-cooked eggs, chopped finely
2–3 tbsp chopped fresh parsley
1 tbsp chopped fresh tarragon, or 1 tsp dried tarragon
2–3 scallions, chopped (optional)
2 tbsp butter or margarine
1 egg, beaten
dried white or golden bread crumbs
salt and pepper
vegetable oil, for brushing or frying

SPICY SAUCE:
⅔ cup dry white wine
⅔ cup tomato ketchup
1–2 garlic cloves, crushed
good dash of Worcestershire sauce

TO GARNISH:
sprigs of fresh parsley
lemon slices

1 Cook the potatoes in boiling, salted water until tender.

2 Meanwhile, put the fish and bay leaf in a saucepan and barely cover with water. Bring to a boil, cover, and simmer for 15 minutes until tender.

3 ▼ Drain the fish, remove the skin and any bones, and flake the flesh. Put in a bowl with the eggs, herbs, scallions, if using, and seasoning, and mix well.

4 ▼ Drain the potatoes, and mash with the butter and seasoning. Add to the fish and mix thoroughly.

5 ▲ Divide the mixture into 8 and shape into cakes. Brush with beaten egg, then coat in bread crumbs. Put on a greased baking sheet, brush with oil and cook in a preheated oven at 400°F for about 30 minutes, until golden. Alternatively, fry for about 5 minutes on each side.

6 To make the spicy sauce, put all the ingredients in a saucepan, bring to a boil, and simmer, uncovered, for about 15 minutes, until thickened and smooth. Adjust the seasoning. Garnish the fish cakes with parsley and lemon, and serve with the sauce.

FLAMENCO EGGS

This Spanish-style egg recipe is full of lively colors and flavors.

SERVES 4

INGREDIENTS:
6 tbsp olive oil
2 thick slices white bread, cut
   into cubes
1 pound potatoes, cut into small cubes
1 onion, chopped
2 ounces green beans, cut into 1-inch
   lengths
2 small zucchini, halved and
   sliced
1 red bell pepper, cored, deseeded, and
   chopped
4 tomatoes, deseeded and sliced
2 chorizo sausages, sliced
chili powder, to taste
4 eggs
salt
chopped fresh parsley,
   to garnish

1 ▼ Heat the oil in a large skillet and add the cubes of bread. Fry until golden brown, then remove with a perforated spoon and drain on paper towels. Set aside.

2 Add the potatoes to the skillet and cook over a low heat, turning often, for about 15 minutes, until they are just tender.

3 ▼ Add the chopped onion to the skillet and cook for 3 minutes, then add the green beans, zucchini, red bell pepper, and tomatoes. Cook gently for 3–4 minutes, stirring often. Stir in the chorizo sausage. Season with salt and a little chili powder.

4 ▼ Grease 4 individual ovenproof dishes, or 1 large ovenproof dish, with olive oil. Transfer the vegetable mixture to the dishes and make a hollow in the mixture. Carefully crack 1 egg into each hollow. Bake in a preheated oven at 375°F for 10 minutes.

5 Sprinkle the cubes of fried bread over the surface and bake for 2 minutes more. Serve immediately, garnished with chopped fresh parsley.

SPANISH OMELET

Use any leftover cooked pasta you may have, such as penne, short-cut macaroni, or shells, to make this fluffy omelet an instant success.

SERVES 2

INGREDIENTS
4 tbsp olive oil
1 small Spanish onion, chopped
1 Florence fennel bulb, thinly sliced
1 cup diced raw potato, dried
1 garlic clove, chopped
4 eggs
1 tbsp chopped fresh parsley
pinch of chili powder
3 ounces short pasta, cooked weight
1 tbsp stuffed green olives, halved, plus
   extra to garnish
salt and pepper
sprigs of fresh marjoram, to garnish
tomato salad, to serve

1 Heat 2 tablespoons of the oil in a heavy-based skillet over a low heat. Fry the onion, fennel, and potato for 8–10 minutes, stirring occasionally, until the potato is just tender. Stir in the garlic and cook for 1 minute. Remove from the heat, lift out the vegetables with a perforated spoon, and set aside. Rinse and dry the pan.

2 Break the eggs into a bowl and beat them until they are frothy. Stir in the parsley, and season with salt, pepper, and chili powder.

3 ▼ Heat 1 tablespoon of the remaining oil in a pan over a medium

heat. Pour in half the beaten eggs, then add the cooked vegetables, the pasta, and the green olives. Pour on the remaining egg and cook until the sides begin to set.

4 ▲ Lift up the edges with a spatula to allow the uncooked egg to spread underneath. Continue cooking the omelet, shaking the pan occasionally, until the underside is golden brown.

5 ▼ Slide the omelet out on to a large, flat plate and wipe the pan clean with paper towels. Heat the remaining oil in the pan and invert the omelet. Cook on the other side until brown.

6 Slide the omelet onto a warmed serving dish. Garnish with a few olives and the marjoram sprigs, and serve hot, cut into wedges and accompanied by a tomato salad.

PICNIC OMELET SQUARES

An oven-baked omelet with diced potatoes, onions, peas, tomatoes, herbs, and cheese is cut into small bite-size squares that are perfect for picnics.

MAKES ABOUT 36 SQUARES

INGREDIENTS:
2 tbsp olive oil
1 onion, thinly sliced
1 garlic clove, crushed
1 zucchini, trimmed and grated coarsely
1 red, green, or orange bell pepper, halved, cored, and deseeded
1 cup diced cooked potato
⅔ cup cooked peas
2 tomatoes, skinned, deseeded, and cut into strips
2 tsp chopped fresh mixed herbs, or 1 tsp dried mixed herbs
6 eggs
⅓–½ cup grated Gruyère or fresh Parmesan cheese
salt and pepper

1 Heat the oil in a large skillet, and fry the onion and garlic very gently for about 5 minutes, until soft but not colored. Add the zucchini and fry for 1–2 minutes more. Transfer the vegetables into a bowl.

2 Place the bell pepper on a broiler rack, skin-side up, and cook under a preheated moderately hot broiler until the skin of the pepper is chargrilled. Let cool slightly, then peel off the blackened skin and slice or chop the bell pepper flesh. Add the bell pepper to the onion mixture, together with the potato, peas, tomatoes, and herbs.

3 ▲ Beat the eggs together with 1–2 tablespoons water and seasoning, then add to the vegetables and mix.

4 ▼ Line a shallow 8–9 inch square cake pan with nonstick parchment

paper. Do not cut into the corners, just fold the parchment paper. Pour in the egg mixture, making sure the vegetables are fairly evenly distributed.

5 Cook in a preheated oven at 350°F for about 15 minutes, or until almost set.

6 ▲ Sprinkle with the cheese and return to the oven for 5–10 minutes, or else place under a preheated moderately hot broiler until evenly browned. Let cool. Remove from the pan, cut into 1–1½ inch squares, and serve immediately. Alternatively, pack the omelet squares for a picnic.

CORNISH PASTIES

Cornish pasties were originally made for miners' lunches in England, which makes them ideal for picnics and packed lunches. For a variation on this recipe, add 1 small chopped carrot to the meat mixture; lamb can also be substituted for the beef in the recipe.

SERVES 4

INGREDIENTS:

12 ounces lean braising steak
4 ounces raw potato, peeled
1 onion
salt and pepper
milk, for brushing

PASTRY:

3 cups all-purpose flour
½ tsp salt
¾ cup margarine, cut into
  small pieces
chilled water,
  to mix

1 ▼ First make the pastry. Sift the flour and salt into a large mixing bowl. Add the margarine and cut in until the mixture resembles fine bread crumbs. Add enough cold water to make a soft, but not sticky, dough. Knead lightly for a few minutes, then wrap the dough well in plastic wrap and chill in the refrigerator for 10–15 minutes.

2 ▼ Divide the dough into 4 pieces. Roll out each piece on a lightly floured work counter to a diameter of about 8 inches.

3 Cut the steak into small pieces, dice the potato, and chop the onion. Mix together in a bowl, and season well with salt and pepper.

4 ▲ Divide the meat mixture equally between the rounds. Dampen the edges with a little water and draw the edges together to form a seam across the top. Crimp the short ends.

5 Place the pasties on a baking sheet and brush with a little milk. Bake in a preheated oven at 425°F for 15 minutes, then reduce the oven temperature to 325°F, cover with foil to prevent them from becoming too brown, and bake for another hour. Serve warm or cold.

ALMOND POTATO BITES

In this recipe, creamy mashed potatoes are coated in crunchy almonds, then fried until golden brown. Serve the potato bites as a party dish, or as a side dish with a special meal.

SERVES 4

INGREDIENTS:
2 pounds main-crop potatoes, peeled and quartered
¼ cup butter
2 tbsp milk
1 egg, beaten
salt and pepper
vegetable oil, for frying

TO COAT:
¼ cup all-purpose flour
salt and pepper
1 egg
2 tbsp cold water
¼ cup blanched almonds, finely chopped

1 Cook the potatoes in plenty of lightly salted, boiling water for 15–20 minutes until tender. Drain well and mash until no large lumps remain.

2 ▼ Add the butter and milk to the potatoes, beating well with a wooden spoon or a hand-held electric mixer. Mix in the beaten egg, and season with salt and pepper.

3 Shape the potato mixture into 20 equal-size small balls or cakes.

4 ▼ Season the flour with salt and pepper, and sprinkle on a flat plate. In a shallow bowl, beat the egg with the cold water. Put the almonds into a separate shallow bowl. Dip the potato balls into the flour, then into the egg, and finally into the almonds to coat evenly.

5 ▲ Pour the vegetable oil into a deep skillet or wok to a depth of ½ inch and heat until a cube of bread browns in 30 seconds. Fry the potato balls in batches for 2–3 minutes, turning often, until golden brown. Lift out with a perforated spoon, drain on paper towels, and serve while hot.

VEGETABLE CHIPS WITH CREAMY GARLIC DIP

These crispy vegetables taste superb and make an excellent snack to serve with drinks.

SERVES 4

INGREDIENTS:
1 large potato, scrubbed
2 large parsnips, scrubbed
6 ounces sweet potato, scrubbed
6 ounces celery root, scrubbed
6 ounces raw beets, scrubbed
vegetable oil, for
    deep frying
salt and pepper

GARLIC DIP:
2 garlic cloves
3–4 scallions, trimmed
few sprigs of mixed fresh herbs, such as
    parsley, chives, dill, marjoram, or
    thyme
1¼ cups sour cream
salt and pepper

1 ▼ Cut all the vegetables into very thin slices, without peeling them. If preferred, this can be done using a food processor or mandoline. Keep the different vegetables in separate batches.

2 Pour the vegetable oil into a deep-fat fryer or wok to a depth of 3–4 inches. Heat the oil to 350–375°F, or until a cube of bread browns in 30 seconds. Fry the vegetables in batches for several minutes until crisp and browned, cooking the red beets last of all to prevent the oil from

discoloring. Lift the crispy vegetable chips from the oil with a perforated spoon and drain on paper towels. Let the chips cool.

3 ▼ Make the dip. Peel and crush the garlic cloves. Finely chop the scallions and herbs.

4 ▲ Put the sour cream in a small mixing bowl, and add the garlic, scallion, and herbs. Season well with salt and pepper. Transfer to a serving bowl, cover, and chill in the refrigerator until ready to serve.

5 Sprinkle the vegetable chips with salt and pepper, and serve with the creamy garlic dip.

SIDE DISHES

Although potatoes are one of the most popular side dishes, there are many more imaginative ways of serving them than most people realize. Potatoes can be cooked by a great number of methods, such as mashing, roasting, stir-frying, pan-frying, deep-frying, baking, and boiling. Some exotic or ethnic-style potato dishes combine well with simply cooked main courses, like broiled fish or chicken, and they can add extra interest to a meal. In this chapter, you will find recipes for all kinds of side dishes, from mashed potatoes, french fries, and new potato or baked potato recipes, to Indian-style side dishes, such as Aloo Chat and Bombay Potatoes, along with the classic French recipe Potatoes Lyonnaise. There are great ideas for adding excitement to old favorites, such as Leek, Mustard & Crispy Bacon Mashed Potatoes or Lemony New Potatoes. There are also recipes for sweet potatoes, such as Sautéed Sweet Potatoes with Rosemary. Be creative when serving different dishes together, and don't be afraid to combine some of the more exotic recipes with dishes from other culinary traditions.

SPICY INDIAN-STYLE POTATOES

Potatoes cooked this way are so delicious, yet quick and simple to prepare. Cut the potatoes into similar-size pieces to make sure they cook evenly.

SERVES 4

INGREDIENTS:

1½ *pounds potatoes*
salt
¼ *cup ghee or clarified butter*
2 tbsp vegetable oil
1 tsp ground turmeric
1 large onion, peeled, quartered, and sliced
2–3 garlic cloves, crushed
2-inch piece fresh ginger, peeled and chopped
1½ tsp cumin seeds
¼–½ *tsp chili powder*
2 tsp lemon juice
1 tbsp shredded fresh mint leaves
sprigs of fresh mint, to garnish

1 ▼ Peel the potatoes and cut into ¼–1 inch cubes. Cook in a pan of boiling, salted water for 6–8 minutes, or until knife-tip tender (do not overcook). Drain well, return to the pan, and shake dry over a moderate heat for a few moments.

2 ▲ Heat the ghee or butter and the oil in a large skillet over a medium heat. Stir in the turmeric, then add the sliced onion and the cooked potatoes. Fry for 4–5 minutes, or until the mixture is beginning to brown, stirring and turning the vegetables frequently.

3 ▼ Stir in the garlic, ginger, cumin seeds, chili powder, and salt to taste. Fry over gentle heat for 1 minute, stirring all the time.

4 Transfer the potatoes to a warm serving dish. Add the lemon juice to the juices in the pan and spoon the mixture over the potatoes. Sprinkle with the shredded mint leaves, garnish with sprigs of mint, and serve hot.

MIXED VEGETABLE BHAJI

In this delicious dish, the vegetables are first parboiled, and then lightly braised with onions, tomatoes, and spices.

SERVES 4–6

INGREDIENTS:
1 small cauliflower
4 ounces green beans
2 potatoes
4 tbsp ghee or vegetable oil
1 onion, chopped
2 garlic cloves, crushed
2-inch piece fresh ginger, peeled and
   cut into fine slivers
1 tsp cumin seeds
2 tbsp medium curry paste
14-ounce can chopped tomatoes
⅔ cup water
4 tbsp strained thick plain yogurt
chopped fresh cilantro,
   to garnish

1 ▼ Break the cauliflower into neat florets. Trim and halve the green beans. Peel and quarter the potatoes lengthwise, then cut each quarter into 3 pieces. Cook all the prepared vegetables in a saucepan of boiling, salted water for 8 minutes. Drain well, return to the pan, and shake dry over a low heat for a few moments.

2 ▼ Heat the ghee or vegetable oil in a large skillet, add the onion, garlic, ginger, and cumin seeds, and stir-fry gently for 3 minutes. Stir in the curry paste, tomatoes, and water, and bring to a boil. Reduce the heat and simmer the spicy mixture for 2 minutes.

3 ▼ Stir in the parboiled vegetables and mix lightly. Cover and cook gently for 5–8 minutes, until just tender and cooked through. Beat the yogurt lightly to soften it and drizzle the vegetable mixture with the yogurt. Sprinkle with the chopped cilantro and serve hot.

FRIED SPICED POTATOES

These spicy potatoes make a super accompaniment to almost any main-course dish, although they are high in calories!

SERVES 4–6

INGREDIENTS:
2 onions, peeled and
　quartered
2-inch piece fresh ginger, peeled
　and finely chopped
2 garlic cloves, peeled
2–3 tbsp mild or medium
　curry paste
4 tbsp water
1½ pounds new potatoes
vegetable oil, for deep frying
3 tbsp vegetable ghee or oil
⅔ cup strained thick plain yogurt
⅔ cup heavy cream
3 tbsp chopped fresh mint
salt and pepper
½ bunch scallions, trimmed and
　chopped, to garnish

1 ▼ Place the onions, ginger, garlic, curry paste, and water in a blender or food processor. Process until smooth, scraping down the sides of the machine, and blending again, if necessary.

2 Cut the potatoes into quarters – the pieces need to be about 1 inch in size – and pat dry with paper towels. Heat the oil in a deep-fat fryer to 350°F, or until a cube of bread browns in 30 seconds. Fry the potatoes, in batches, for about 5 minutes, or until golden brown, turning frequently. Remove the potatoes from the oil and drain on paper towels.

3 ▼ Heat the ghee or oil in a large skillet, add the curry and onion mixture, and fry gently for 2 minutes, stirring all the time. Add the yogurt, cream, and 2 tablespoons of the fresh mint. Mix well.

4 ▼ Add the fried potatoes and stir until coated in the sauce. Cook for 5–7 minutes more, or until heated through and sauce has thickened, stirring frequently.

5 Season with salt and pepper to taste, and sprinkle with the remaining chopped mint and sliced scallions. Serve immediately.

CURRIED ROAST POTATOES

This is the kind of Indian-inspired dish that would fit easily into any Western menu. Delicious on a buffet, or as a surprise accompaniment to a dinner of roast meat, it would also be good served with a curry instead of the more traditional rice.

SERVES 4

INGREDIENTS:
2 tsp cumin seeds
2 tsp coriander seeds
⅓ cup salted butter
1 tsp ground turmeric
1 tsp black mustard seeds
2 garlic cloves, crushed
2 dried red chilies
1½ pounds baby new potatoes

1 ▼ Grind the cumin and coriander seeds together in a mortar and pestle, or a spice grinder. Grinding them fresh like this captures all of the flavor before it has a chance to dry out.

2 Melt the butter gently in a roasting pan, and add the turmeric, mustard seeds, garlic, and chilies, and the ground cumin and coriander seeds. Stir well to combine evenly. Place in a preheated oven at 400°F for 5 minutes.

3 ▼ Remove the roasting pan from the oven – the spices should be very fragrant at this stage – and add the potatoes. Stir well so the butter and spice mix coats the potatoes completely.

4 ▲ Put back in the preheated oven and bake for 20–25 minutes, stirring occasionally. Test the potatoes with a skewer – if they drop off the end of the skewer when lifted, they are done. Serve immediately.

ALOO CHAT

Aloo Chat (chat means salad) is one of a variety of Indian foods served at any time of the day. Indians are expert at combining flavors and textures in subtle mixes designed to satisfy and stimulate the appetite. This makes an exciting side dish that can be served with all kinds of dishes, not just Indian food.

SERVES 4

INGREDIENTS:
generous ¼ cup garbanzo beans, soaked overnight in cold water and drained
1 dried red chili
1 pound waxy potatoes, such as red-skinned or round white potatoes, boiled in their skins and peeled
1 tsp cumin seeds
1 tsp black peppercorns
2 tsp salt
¼ tsp dried mint
¼ tsp chili powder
¼ tsp ground ginger
2 tsp mango powder
¼ cup plain yogurt
vegetable oil, for deep frying
4 poppadoms

1 ▼ Boil the garbanzo beans with the dried red chilli in plenty of water for about 1 hour, until tender. Drain well.

2 ▲ Cut the potatoes into 1-inch dice and mix into the garbanzo beans in a large bowl while the beans are still warm. Set aside.

3 Grind together the cumin, peppercorns, and salt in a spice grinder or mortar and pestle. Stir in the dried mint, chili powder, ginger, and mango powder.

4 ▼ Put a small dry saucepan or skillet over a low heat and add the spice mix. Stir until fragrant and immediately remove from the heat.

5 Stir half of the spice mix into the bowl with the garbanzo beans and potatoes, and stir the yogurt into the other half.

6 Cook the poppadoms according to the instructions on the package. Drain on plenty of paper towels. Break into bite-size pieces and stir into the potatoes and garbanzo beans. Spoon the spiced yogurt over the top and serve immediately.

BOMBAY POTATOES

Although virtually unknown in India, this dish is a very popular item on Indian restaurant menus in other parts of the world. It works best when served with rice as a vegetable dish, rather than replacing the rice in a meal. The success of the recipe rests on using waxy potatoes, such as round white potatoes, because they do not break up readily. Panch poran spice mix, which includes cumin, fennel, nigella, and fenugreek, can be bought from Asian or Indian food stores.

SERVES 4

INGREDIENTS:
2 pounds waxy potatoes, peeled
2 tbsp ghee
1 tsp panch poran spice mix
3 tsp ground turmeric
2 tbsp tomato paste
1¼ cups plain yogurt
salt
chopped fresh cilantro,
  to garnish

1 Put the whole potatoes into a large saucepan of salted cold water, bring to a boil, then simmer until the potatoes are just cooked but not tender; the time depends on the size of the potato, but an average-size one should take about 15 minutes.

2 ▲ Put the ghee into a saucepan over a medium heat, and add the panch poran, turmeric, tomato paste, yogurt, and salt. Bring to a boil and simmer, uncovered, for 5 minutes.

3 ▲ Drain the potatoes and cut each into 4 pieces.

4 Add the potatoes to the pan and cook with a lid on. Transfer to an ovenproof casserole dish, cover, and cook in a preheated oven at 350°F for about 40 minutes, until the potatoes are tender and the sauce has thickened a little.

5 ▲ Sprinkle liberally with fresh chopped cilantro and serve.

MUSTARD & ONION POTATOES

Mustard seeds give the potatoes a nutty taste. This dish can be served with any type of main course, and is especially good served with curries or with grilled kebabs in the summer.

SERVES 4

INGREDIENTS:
12 ounces small new potatoes
3 tbsp oil
2 tbsp brown mustard seeds
1 tsp cumin seeds
1 tsp crushed dried red chilies
8 ounces baby onions
1 garlic clove, chopped
½-inch piece fresh ginger
¼ tsp garam masala

1 ▲ Boil the potatoes in salted water for 10–15 minutes, until just tender. Drain the potatoes, cut in half if they are large, and set aside.

2 ▼ Heat the oil in a Balti pan or wok, add the mustard seeds, cumin, and chilies, and fry until the seeds start to pop.

3 ▼ Add the onions to the pan and stir-fry until golden brown. Add the garlic and ginger, and stir-fry for 1 minute longer.

4 ▼ Stir in the potatoes and garam masala, and stir-fry for 4–5 minutes, until the potatoes are golden brown. Serve hot.

POTATOES LYONNAISE

In this classic French recipe, sliced potatoes are cooked with onions to make a delicious accompaniment to a main meal. If you find that the potatoes blacken slightly as they boil, add a teaspoonful of lemon juice to the cooking water.

SERVES 4

INGREDIENTS
2¼ pounds main-crop potatoes,
   peeled
4 tbsp olive oil
2 tbsp butter
2 onions, sliced
2–3 garlic cloves, crushed (optional)
salt and pepper
chopped fresh parsley, to garnish

1 Slice the potatoes into ⅜-inch slices. Put in a large saucepan of lightly salted water and bring to a boil. Cover and simmer gently for 10–12 minutes, until just tender. Avoid boiling too rapidly or else the potatoes will break up and lose their shape. When cooked, drain well.

2 ▲ While the potatoes are cooking, heat the oil and butter in a very large skillet, and sauté the onions and the garlic, if using, until the onions are softened.

3 ▼ Add the cooked potatoes to the skillet and cook with the onions, stirring occasionally, for 5–8 minutes. until the potatoes are well-browned all over.

4 ▲ Season well. Sprinkle over the chopped parsley to serve. If wished, transfer the potatoes and onions to a large ovenproof dish and keep warm in a low oven until ready to serve.

LEMONY NEW POTATOES & HERBY NEW POTATOES

Choose from these two divine recipes for new potatoes. To check that new potatoes are fresh, rub the skin; the skin will come off easily if fresh.

SERVES 4

LEMONY NEW POTATO INGREDIENTS:

2 pounds new potatoes
3 tbsp butter
1 tbsp finely grated lemon rind
2 tbsp lemon juice
1 tbsp chopped fresh dill or chives
salt and pepper
extra chopped fresh dill or chives,
   to garnish

1 ▼ Scrub the potatoes well, or remove skins by scraping off with a sharp knife. Cook the potatoes in plenty of lightly salted, boiling water for about 15 minutes, until just tender.

2 ▼ While the potatoes are cooking, melt the butter over a low heat. Add the lemon rind, juice, and herbs. Season with salt and pepper.

3 Drain the cooked potatoes and transfer to a serving bowl. Pour over the lemony butter mixture and stir gently to mix. Garnish with extra herbs and serve hot or warm.

HERBY NEW POTATO INGREDIENTS:

2 pounds new potatoes
3 tbsp light olive oil
1½ tbsp white wine vinegar
pinch of dry mustard
pinch of superfine sugar
salt and pepper
2 tbsp chopped mixed fresh herbs, such
   as parsley, chives, marjoram, basil,
   and rosemary
extra chopped fresh mixed herbs,
   to garnish

1 Prepare and cook the potatoes as described in step 1 above.

2 While the potatoes are cooking, beat the oil, vinegar, mustard, superfine sugar, and seasoning together in a small bowl. Add the chopped herbs and mix well to combine.

3 ▲ Drain the potatoes and pour over the oil and vinegar mixture, stirring to coat evenly.

4 Transfer to a serving bowl. Garnish with extra fresh herbs and serve the potatoes warm or cold.

MASHED POTATOES WITH MELTED CHEESE & LEEK, MUSTARD, & CRISPY BACON

Creamy mashed potato is a favorite with so many meals. Here are two tasty versions to try.

SERVES 4

MELTED CHEESE INGREDIENTS:
2 pounds main-crop potatoes, peeled
salt and pepper
2 tbsp butter
1–2 garlic cloves, crushed
4 tbsp milk
¼ cup grated mozzarella or cheddar cheese

1 Cut the potatoes into quarters and cook in lightly salted, boiling water for about 20 minutes, until tender. Drain well, mash, and season.

2 ▲ Melt the butter in a small skillet and sauté the garlic for about 3 minutes, until softened. Add to the potatoes with the milk and beat well with a wooden spoon, or use a hand-held electric mixer, until the potatoes are smooth and creamy.

3 ▼ Transfer to a greased ovenproof dish. Sprinkle with the cheese and bake in a preheated oven at 350°F for 15–20 minutes.

LEEK, MUSTARD, AND CRISPY BACON INGREDIENTS:
2 pounds main-crop potatoes, peeled
salt and pepper
2 tbsp butter
1 large leek, chopped
2 tsp coarse-grain mustard
4 slices bacon
chopped fresh parsley, to garnish

1 Prepare, boil, and mash the potatoes as described for the Melted Cheese version, seasoning well with salt and pepper.

2 ▲ Melt the butter in a small skillet and sauté the leek until softened. Add to the mashed potatoes with the mustard. Transfer to a greased ovenproof dish and bake in a preheated oven at 350°F for 15–20 minutes.

3 While cooking, broil the bacon under a preheated hot broiler until crisp. Remove, drain on paper towels, and snip into bacon bits. Scatter the bacon bits and parsley over the mashed potatoes and serve.

FLUFFY BAKED POTATOES

With just a little extra effort, baked potatoes can taste magnificent! Chopped red bell pepper and drained canned corn kernels can be used instead of ham for a vegetarian alternative.

SERVES 4

INGREDIENTS:
4 large baking potatoes, scrubbed
¼ cup chopped cooked ham
1 cup grated cheddar or red Leicester
   cheese
2 tsp coarse-grain mustard
2 eggs, separated
salt and pepper
sprigs of fresh parsley, to garnish

1 Use a fork to prick the potatoes 2 or 3 times to prevent them from bursting. Bake in a preheated oven at 400°F for about 1 hour, until tender. Alternatively, cook for 10–12 minutes in a microwave oven on high power. Let the potatoes cool for a few minutes after cooking.

2 ▲ Halve the potatoes and carefully scoop out the flesh into a large bowl, being careful to avoid damaging the skins. Mash the potato flesh by hand with a fork or masher, until no large lumps remain.

3 ▼ Mix the ham, cheese, mustard, and egg yolks into the mashed potato, stirring well to combine. Season with salt and pepper.

4 ▲ Beat the egg whites in a bowl until stiff. Using a large metal spoon, gently fold the egg whites into the potato mixture.

5 Spoon the mixture back into the potato skins and place in a shallow, greased baking dish. Bake for 15–20 minutes more, until the potatoes are set and golden brown on top. Garnish with the parsley sprigs and serve.

SAUTÉED SWEET POTATOES WITH ROSEMARY

Sweet potatoes are used in this recipe to make a tasty side dish, but you can substitute ordinary potatoes, if wished.

SERVES 4

INGREDIENTS:
⅔ cup light cream
1 tsp lemon juice
1 tbsp snipped fresh chives
2 pounds sweet potatoes, scrubbed
1 tsp salt
4 tbsp olive oil
1 tbsp butter
1 tbsp chopped fresh rosemary
¼ tsp allspice
salt and pepper
sprigs of fresh rosemary, to garnish

1 Pour the cream into a small serving bowl. Stir in the lemon juice to combine. Cover and refrigerate for 20–30 minutes to "sour" the cream. Add the chives and stir to mix. Refrigerate until ready to serve.

2 ▼ Put the sweet potatoes into a large saucepan of cold water. Add the salt and bring to a boil. Cover, reduce the heat, and simmer for about 15 minutes, until just tender. Drain well, then peel and dice.

3 ▼ Heat the oil and butter in a large skillet, and add the diced sweet potatoes. Sauté the potatoes over a medium heat for about 8 minutes, stirring occasionally, until they are golden brown.

4 ▲ Add the rosemary to the sweet potatoes. Season the mixture with allspice, salt, and pepper. Garnish with sprigs of rosemary and serve while hot, accompanied by the sour cream.

FRENCH FRIES

This recipe makes perfect french fries – light, crisp, and golden brown. You may like to use a mandoline or food processor to cut the potatoes into different shapes for added interest. Unpeeled potatoes can also be used; just scrub well before cutting to size.

SERVES 4

✿✿✿✿✿✿✿✿✿✿✿✿✿✿✿✿✿

INGREDIENTS:
*2 pounds main-crop potatoes, peeled
vegetable oil, for frying
salt and pepper*

✿✿✿✿✿✿✿✿✿✿✿✿✿✿✿✿✿

1 Cut the potatoes into ½-inch slices, and then into ½-inch wide strips. Rinse well in cold water, drain thoroughly, and pat dry with paper towels. (If preparing ahead of time, place the cut potatoes in a large bowl and cover with cold water until ready to cook.)

2 ▲ Add the vegetable oil to a depth of 3–4 inches in a deep-fat fryer. Heat to a temperature of 350–375°F. To test that the oil is hot enough, add one potato slice; it should rise to the surface, surrounded by bubbles, when the oil is hot enough. Add enough raw potato slices to quarter-fill the wire basket. Carefully lower the basket into the oil and cook for about 6 minutes.

3 ▼ Lift the wire basket from the oil and drain for a few seconds. Remove the french fries and drain on paper towels. Repeat the procedure until all the potatoes are cooked.

4 ▲ Just before serving, reheat the oil and deep-fry the fries for 3–4 minutes more, until crisp and golden brown. Drain well on paper towels, season with salt and pepper, and serve.

MAIN MEALS

Potatoes find their way into almost every meal, whether they are included in the main dish or served on the side. On the following pages, you will find a range of recipes for main meals, some which include potatoes as one of the ingredients and others which are served with special potato recipes. Although there are delicious dishes for lamb, fish, chicken, and beef, there are also some fabulous recipes that are suitable for vegetarians, such as Croustades with Sunshine Bell Peppers and Potato Gnocchi with Garlic & Herb Sauce. The recipes are diverse, too, influenced by many different cuisines from around the world, such as the Indian Easy Lamb & Potato Masala and Mexican Baked Tortillas. There are recipes to suit all tastes and occasions, from hearty main courses like as Irish Stew and Beef & Potato Goulash, to lighter meals like the Cheese & Onion Quiche and Soused Trout. Whether you are cooking for one or two, a family or a number of guests at a dinner party, you will find something here to interest you.

EASY LAMB & POTATO MASALA

It's so easy to create delicious Indian dishes at home – simply open a can of curry sauce, add a few interesting ingredients, and you have a splendid dish that is sure to be popular with family or friends.

SERVES 4

INGREDIENTS:

1½ pounds lean lamb (from the leg)
4 tbsp ghee or vegetable oil
1 pound potatoes, peeled and cut in
   large 1-inch pieces
1 large onion, quartered and sliced
2 garlic cloves, crushed
6 ounces mushrooms, thickly sliced
10-ounce can commercial variety of
   tikka masala curry sauce
1¼ cups water
salt
3 tomatoes, halved and cut into thin
   slices
4 ounces spinach, washed and stalks
   trimmed
cooked rice, to serve
sprigs of fresh mint, to garnish

1 ▼ Cut the lamb into 1-inch cubes. Heat the ghee or oil in a large pan, add the lamb, and fry over moderate heat for 3 minutes, or until sealed all over. Remove from the pan.

2 ▼ Add the potatoes, onion, garlic, and mushrooms, and fry for 3–4 minutes, stirring frequently. Stir the curry sauce and water into the pan, add the lamb, mix well, and season with salt to taste. Cover and cook very slowly for 1 hour, or until the lamb is tender and cooked through, stirring occasionally.

3 ▲ Add the sliced tomatoes and the spinach to the pan, pushing the leaves down into the mixture. Cover the pan and cook the curry mixture for 10 minutes more, until the spinach is cooked and tender.

4 Serve on a bed of rice, garnished with mint sprigs.

ROSEMARY & RED CURRANT LAMB WITH LEEK MASHED POTATOES

This is a pretty dish of pink tender lamb served on a light green bed of mashed leeks and potatoes.

SERVES 4

INGREDIENTS:
1 pound lean lamb tenderloin
4 tbsp red currant jelly
1 tbsp chopped fresh rosemary
1 garlic clove, crushed
4 cups diced potatoes
1 pound leeks, sliced
¼ cup fresh vegetable stock
4 tsp low-fat fromage blanc
salt and pepper
freshly steamed vegetables,
  to serve

TO GARNISH:
chopped fresh rosemary
fresh red currants

1 ▼ Put the lamb tenderloin in a shallow baking pan. Blend 2 tablespoons of the red currant jelly with the rosemary, garlic, and seasoning. Brush over the lamb and cook in a preheated oven at 450°F for 30 minutes, brushing occasionally with any cooking juices.

2 Meanwhile, place the potatoes in a saucepan and cover with water. Bring to a boil and cook for 8 minutes, until soft. Drain well. Put the leeks in a saucepan with the stock. Cover and simmer for 7–8 minutes, until soft. Drain, reserving the cooking liquid.

3 ▲ Place the potato and leeks in a bowl and mash them. Season to taste and stir in the fromage blanc. Pile onto a warm platter and keep warm.

4 ▼ In a saucepan, melt the remaining red currant jelly and stir in the leek cooking liquid. Bring the mixture to a boil for 5 minutes, until reduced to a sauce.

5 Slice the lamb and arrange over the leek mashed potatoes. Spoon the red currant sauce over the top. Garnish with chopped rosemary and red currants, and serve immediately with freshly steamed vegetables.

SOUSED TROUT

In this recipe, fillets of trout are gently poached in a spiced vinegar, left to marinate for 24 hours, and served cold with a potato salad.

SERVES 4

INGREDIENTS:
4 trout, about 28–12 ounces each, filleted
1 onion, sliced very thinly
2 bay leaves, preferably fresh
sprigs of fresh parsley and dill, or other fresh herbs
10–12 black peppercorns
4–6 cloves
good pinch of salt
⅔ cup red wine vinegar
mixed salad leaves, to garnish

POTATO SALAD:
1 pound small new potatoes
2 tbsp French dressing
4 tbsp mayonnaise
3–4 scallions, sliced

1 ▼ Trim the trout fillets, cutting off any pieces of fin. If preferred, remove the skin – use a sharp knife and, beginning at the tail end, carefully cut the flesh from the skin, pressing the knife down firmly as you work.

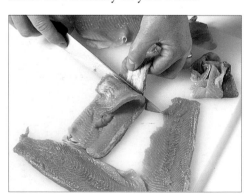

2 Lightly grease a shallow ovenproof dish and lay the fish in it, packing them fairly tightly together but keeping them in a single layer. Arrange the sliced onion, bay leaves, and herbs over the fish.

3 ▲ Put the peppercorns, cloves, salt, and vinegar into a saucepan, and bring almost to a boil. Remove from the heat and pour evenly over the fish.

4 Cover with foil and cook in a preheated oven at 325°F for 15 minutes. Leave until cold, and then refrigerate to chill completely.

5 Meanwhile, make the potato salad. Cook the potatoes in boiling, salted water for 10–15 minutes, until just tender. Drain. While still warm, cut into large dice and place in a bowl.

6 ▼ Combine the French dressing and mayonnaise, add to the potatoes while warm, and toss evenly. Leave until cold, then sprinkle with the chopped scallions.

7 Serve each portion of fish with a little of the juices, garnished with salad leaves and accompanied by the potato salad.

CROUSTADES WITH SUNSHINE BELL PEPPERS

This colorful combination of grated vegetables and mixed bell peppers would make a stunning impression on dinner guests.

SERVES 4

INGREDIENTS:
1 orange bell pepper
1 red bell pepper
1 yellow bell pepper
3 tbsp olive oil
2 tbsp red wine vinegar
1 tsp French mustard
1 tsp clear honey
salt and pepper
sprigs of fresh flat-leaf parsley, to garnish
green vegetables, to serve

CROUSTADES:
8 ounces potatoes, grated coarsely
8 ounces carrots, grated coarsely
12 ounces celery root, grated coarsely
1 garlic clove, crushed
1 tbsp lemon juice
2 tbsp butter or margarine, melted
1 egg, beaten
1 tbsp vegetable oil

1 Place the bell peppers on a baking sheet and bake in a preheated oven at 375° for 35 minutes, turning after 20 minutes.

2 ▼ Cover with a clean dish cloth and let cool for 10 minutes. Peel the skin from the cooked bell peppers. Cut

each bell pepper in half, and discard the core and seeds. Thinly slice the flesh into strips and place them in a shallow dish.

3 Put the oil, vinegar, mustard, honey, and seasoning in a small screw-topped jar and shake well to mix. Pour the dressing over the bell pepper strips, mix well, and leave to marinate for 2 hours.

4 ▲ To make the croustades, put the grated potatoes, carrots, and celery root in a large mixing bowl. Toss in the garlic and lemon juice and mix well.

5 ▼ Mix in the melted butter or margarine and the egg. Season well. Divide the mixture into 8 and pile onto 2 baking sheets lined with parchment paper, shaping each into a 4-inch round. Brush with oil.

6 Bake in a preheated oven at 425°F for 30–35 minutes, until crisp around the edge and golden. Carefully transfer to a warm serving dish. Heat the bell peppers and marinade for 2–3 minutes, until warmed through. Spoon the bell peppers over the croustades, garnish with parsley sprigs, and serve with the green vegetables.

POTATO GNOCCHI WITH GARLIC & HERB SAUCE

These little potato dumplings are a traditional Italian appetizer, but they make a substantial meal when served with a salad and bread. If you want to serve them as an appetizer, they would serve six people.

SERVES 4

INGREDIENTS:
2 pounds main-crop potatoes, cut into ½-inch pieces
¼ cup butter or margarine
1 egg, beaten
2¼ cups all-purpose flour
salt

GARLIC AND HERB SAUCE:
½ cup olive oil
2 garlic cloves, chopped very finely
1 tbsp chopped fresh oregano
1 tbsp chopped fresh basil
salt and pepper

TO SERVE:
freshly grated Parmesan cheese (optional)
mixed salad
warm ciabatta

1 Cook the potatoes in boiling, salted water for about 10 minutes, or until tender. Drain well.

2 ▼ Press the hot potatoes through a strainer into a large bowl. Add 1 teaspoon of salt, the butter or margarine, egg, and 1¼ cups of the flour. Mix to bind together.

3 Turn onto a lightly floured work counter and knead, gradually adding the remaining flour, until a smooth, soft, slightly sticky dough is formed.

4 ▼ Flour the hands and roll the dough into ¾-inch thick rolls. Cut into ½-inch pieces. Press the top of each one with the floured prongs of a fork and spread out on a clean floured dish cloth.

5 ▲ Bring a large saucepan of salted water to a simmer. Add the gnocchi and cook in batches for 2–3 minutes, until they rise to the surface.

6 Remove with a perforated spoon and put in a warm, greased serving dish. Cover and keep warm.

7 To make the sauce, put the oil, garlic, and seasoning in a saucepan and cook gently, stirring, for 3–4 minutes, until the garlic is golden. Remove from the heat and stir in the herbs. Pour over the gnocchi and serve immediately, sprinkled with Parmesan, if liked, and accompanied by salad and warm ciabatta bread.

POTATO PIZZA BASE

This is an unusual pizza base made from mashed potatoes and flour, and it is a great way to use up any leftover boiled potatoes. Children love this base, and you will soon have them asking for more.

MAKES ONE 10-INCH ROUND BASE

❈❈❈❈❈❈❈❈❈❈❈❈

INGREDIENTS:
8 ounces boiled potatoes
¼ cup butter or margarine
1 cup self-rising flour
¼ tsp salt

❈❈❈❈❈❈❈❈❈❈❈❈

1 ▼ If the potatoes are hot, mash them, then stir in the butter until it has melted and is distributed evenly throughout the potatoes. Let the mashed potatoes cool.

2 ▼ Sift the flour and salt together, and stir into the mashed potato to form a soft dough.

3 If the potatoes are cold, mash them without adding the butter. Sift the flour and salt into a separate mixing bowl.

4 ▼ Cut the butter into small manageable pieces and cut in to the mashed potatoes with your fingertips, until the mixture resembles fine bread crumbs. Stir the flour and salt mixture into the mashed potatoes to form a soft dough.

5 ▲ Either roll out or press the dough into a 10-inch circle on a lightly greased baking sheet or pizza pan, pushing up the edge slightly to form a ridge. This base is tricky to lift before it is cooked, so you will find it easier to roll it out on the baking sheet.

6 If the base is not needed for cooking immediately, cover it with plastic wrap and chill in the refrigerator for up to 2 hours.

TOMATO SAUCE

This sauce is made with fresh tomatoes. Use the plum variety whenever available, and always choose the reddest tomatoes to give a better color and sweetness to the sauce. When plum tomatoes are readily available, make several batches of the sauce and freeze them.

MAKES ENOUGH TO COVER ONE 10-INCH PIZZA BASE

INGREDIENTS:
1 small onion, chopped
1 small red bell pepper, cored, deseeded and chopped
1 garlic clove, crushed
2 tbsp olive oil
8 ounces tomatoes
1 tbsp tomato paste
1 tsp soft brown sugar
2 tsp chopped fresh basil
¼ tsp dried oregano
1 bay leaf
salt and pepper

1 ▼ Sauté the onion, bell pepper, and garlic in the oil for 5 minutes, until softened but not browned.

2 ▲ Cut a cross in the base of each tomato and place in a bowl. Pour on boiling water and leave for 45 seconds. Drain, and then plunge in cold water. The skins will slide off easily.

3 ▼ Chop the tomatoes, discarding any hard cores. Add the chopped

tomatoes, tomato paste, sugar, herbs, and seasoning to the onion mixture. Stir well. Bring to a boil, cover, and simmer gently for 30 minutes, stirring occasionally, until a thickish sauce is produced.

4 ▼ Remove the bay leaf and adjust the seasoning to taste. Let cool completely before using.

5 This sauce will keep well in a screw-topped jar in the refrigerator for up to a week.

GARDINIERE PIZZA WITH POTATO BASE

As the name implies, this colorful pizza should be topped with fresh vegetables grown in the garden, but because many of us do not have space to grow anything more than a few flowers, we have to rely on other sources. The vegetables used here are only a suggestion; you can replace them with the same quantity of any other vegetable you have available.

SERVES 2–4

INGREDIENTS:
6 fresh spinach leaves
1 Potato Base (see page 75)
1 quantity Tomato Sauce
  (see page 76)
1 tomato, sliced
1 celery stalk, sliced thinly
¼ green bell pepper, sliced thinly
1 baby zucchini, sliced
1 ounce asparagus tips
¼ cup corn kernels, defrosted
  if frozen
¼ cup peas, defrosted if frozen
4 scallions, trimmed and
  chopped
1 tbsp chopped fresh mixed herbs, such
  as tarragon and parsley
½ cup grated mozzarella cheese
2 tbsp grated fresh Parmesan cheese
1 artichoke heart
olive oil, for drizzling
salt and pepper

1 ▼ Remove any stalks from the spinach and wash the leaves in plenty of cold water. Pat dry with paper towels.

2 ▼ Roll out or press the potato base, using a rolling pin or your hands, into a large 10-inch circle on a large, greased baking sheet or pizza pan, and push up the edge a little to form a rim. Spread with the Tomato Sauce.

3 ▼ Arrange the spinach on the sauce, followed by the tomatoes. Top with the remaining vegetables and herbs.

4 ▼ Mix together the mozzarella and Parmesan cheeses in a separate bowl, then sprinkle over the pizza. Place the artichoke heart in the center. Drizzle the pizza with a little olive oil and season well.

5 Bake in a preheated oven at 400°F for 18–20 minutes, or until the edges are crisp and golden. Serve immediately.

MEXICAN BAKED TORTILLAS WITH TOMATO SALSA

Soft flour tortillas are filled with potatoes, bell peppers, and refried beans. If refried beans are not available, substitute red kidney beans.

SERVES 4

INGREDIENTS:
3 tbsp vegetable oil
1 onion, chopped
1–2 garlic cloves, crushed
⅓ green bell pepper, cored, deseeded, and chopped
⅓ red bell pepper, cored, deseeded, and chopped
3 cups diced cooked potato
⅓ large fresh green chili, deseeded and finely chopped
1 tbsp chopped fresh cilantro
7-ounce can refried beans
salt and pepper
4 soft flour tortillas
1 cup grated cheddar cheese
sprigs of fresh cilantro, to garnish

TOMATO SALSA:
⅓ cup tomato juice
4 tomatoes, finely chopped
2-inch piece cucumber, finely chopped
1 small onion, finely chopped
1 tbsp chopped fresh cilantro

1 ▼ Heat the oil in a large skillet and sauté the onion and garlic until softened. Add the bell peppers, potatoes, and chili, and cook for 3–4 minutes more, until browned.

2 ▼ Add the cilantro and refried beans to the skillet and mix well. Stir until completely heated through. Season with salt and pepper.

3 Lay the flour tortillas on a work counter and divide the filling equally between them. Carefully roll up each tortilla and place them in a greased baking dish, with folded sides up. Scatter the grated cheese on top and bake in a preheated oven at 350°F for 20–25 minutes.

4 ▼ Meanwhile, mix all the salsa ingredients together in a small mixing bowl, seasoning well. Refrigerate until ready to serve.

5 Garnish the baked tortillas with sprigs of fresh cilantro and serve hot, accompanied by the salsa.

CHEESE & ONION QUICHE

This quiche is made with a potato "pastry" shell, which is filled with a tasty cheese and onion mixture. To add a stronger flavor of cheese, add 2 tablespoons of grated Parmesan to the filling mixture.

SERVES 6

INGREDIENTS:
2 large onions, chopped
1½ cups grated cheddar cheese
3 eggs, beaten
salt and pepper
1 tbsp chopped fresh parsley
  or chives

POTATO PASTRY:
1½ pounds main-crop potatoes,
  peeled
1 tbsp butter
½ cup all-purpose flour
1 egg, beaten
salt and pepper

1 Prepare the pastry. Put the potatoes in a saucepan of lightly salted, boiling water and boil for 20 minutes, until tender. Drain well and mash until no lumps remain.

2 ▼ Mix the butter, flour, and egg into the mashed potato. Season well with salt and pepper.

3 ▼ Turn the potato pastry into a 10-inch quiche pan. Using floured hands, press the pastry over the base and up the sides of the pan. Prick the base all over with a fork. Line the pastry shell with foil and bake in a preheated oven at 400°F for 15 minutes.

4 Meanwhile, cook the onions in a small amount of boiling water for about 10 minutes, until just tender. Drain the onions well and return to the pan.

5 ▲ Mix the grated cheese into the onions and stir to melt. Cool slightly, then stir in the beaten eggs. Season well and add the parsley or chives.

6 Remove the pastry shell from the oven and remove the foil. Let cool for 10 minutes. Reduce the oven temperature to 375°F.

7 Pour the cheesy onion mixture into the shell. Return to the oven and bake for 25–30 minutes, until the quiche is set and golden brown.

BEEF & POTATO GOULASH

Potatoes are the most natural accompaniment to goulash, and in this recipe, they are actually cooked in the goulash! For a change, you may prefer to substitute small, scrubbed new potatoes for the ordinary potatoes in the recipe.

SERVES 4

INGREDIENTS:
2 tablespoons vegetable oil
1 large onion, sliced
2 garlic cloves, crushed
1½ pounds chuck or stewing steak, cut into pieces
2 tbsp paprika
14-ounce can chopped tomatoes
2 tbsp tomato paste
1 large red bell pepper, cored, deseeded, and chopped
6 ounces mushrooms, wiped and sliced
2½ cups beef stock
1 pound potatoes, peeled and cut into large chunks
1 tbsp cornstarch
salt and pepper

TO GARNISH:
4 tbsp plain yogurt
paprika
chopped fresh parsley

2 ▼ Add the paprika to the pan and stir well. Add the tomatoes, tomato paste, red bell pepper, and mushrooms. Cook for about 2 minutes, stirring constantly.

4 Add the potatoes and cook, covered, for 20–30 minutes more, until tender.

1 ▼ Heat the oil in a large saucepan and sauté the onion and garlic for 3–4 minutes until softened. Add the pieces of steak and cook over a high heat for about 3 minutes, until browned all over.

3 Pour in the stock. Bring to a boil, then reduce the heat. Cover and simmer for about 1½ hours, until the meat is tender.

5 ▲ Blend the cornstarch with a little water and add to the saucepan, stirring until thickened and blended. Cook for about 1 minute, then season with salt and pepper. Top with the plain yogurt, sprinkle over the paprika and chopped fresh parsley, and serve immediately.

SPANISH CHICKEN CASSEROLE

Tomatoes, olives, peppers, and potatoes, with a splash of Spanish red wine, make this marvelous peasant-style dish. The olives mellow during cooking to give a delicious subtle flavor.

SERVES 4

INGREDIENTS:

¼ cup all-purpose flour
1 tsp salt
pepper
1 tbsp paprika
4 chicken portions
3 tbsp olive oil
1 large onion, chopped
2 garlic cloves, crushed
6 tomatoes, chopped, or a 14-ounce can chopped tomatoes
1 green bell pepper, cored, deseeded, and chopped
⅔ cup Spanish red wine
1¼ cups chicken stock
3 medium potatoes, peeled and quartered
12 pitted black olives
1 bay leaf
crusty bread, to serve

1 Put the flour, salt, pepper, and paprika into a large plastic bag. Rinse the chicken portions, put them into the bag, and shake to coat in the seasoned flour.

2 ▼ Heat the oil in a large flameproof casserole dish. Add the chicken portions and cook over a

medium–high heat for 5–8 minutes, until well-browned on each side. Lift out of the casserole with a perforated spoon and set aside.

3 ▼ Add the onion and garlic to the casserole, and cook for a few minutes until browned. Add the tomatoes and bell pepper, and cook for 2–3 minutes more.

4 ▼ Return the chicken to the casserole. Add the wine, stock, and potatoes, and then the olives and bay leaf. Cover and bake in a preheated oven at 375°F for 1 hour, until the chicken is tender.

5 Check the seasoning, adding more salt and pepper if necessary. Serve hot with chunks of crusty bread.

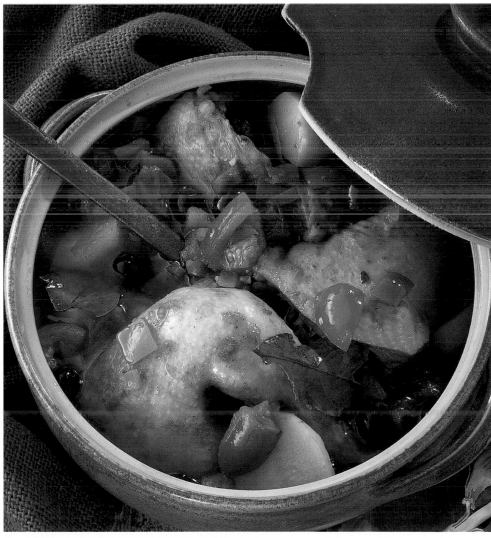

IRISH STEW WITH PARSLEY DUMPLINGS

This traditional recipe makes a hearty stew with fluffy parsley dumplings, but you can make it without the dumplings and serve it with crusty bread instead. Cubes of lean lamb shoulder could be used in place of the cutlets.

SERVES 4

INGREDIENTS:
2 tbsp vegetable oil
2 large onions, sliced
1 leek, sliced
1 large carrot, sliced
2 celery stalks, sliced
3¾ cups lamb stock
1½ pounds lean lamb cutlets, trimmed
⅓ cup pearl barley
2 large potatoes, peeled and cut into large chunks
salt and pepper
chopped fresh parsley, to garnish

DUMPLINGS:
¾ cup self-rising flour
¼ cup rolled oats
2 tbsp chopped fresh parsley
pinch of salt
2 ounces suet
chilled water, to mix

1 ▼ First make the dumplings. Put the flour, oats, parsley, and salt into a large mixing bowl. Stir in the suet. Add enough chilled water to make a soft, but not sticky, dough. Shape into 8 dumplings, cover with a clean dish cloth, and set aside.

2 ▼ Heat the vegetable oil in a large saucepan and sauté the onions, leek, carrot, and celery for 5 minutes, without browning.

3 Add the stock, lamb, and pearl barley to the saucepan. Bring to a boil, and then reduce the heat. Cover and simmer for 30–40 minutes, adding the potatoes after 20 minutes.

4 ▲ Add the dumplings to the saucepan. Cover and simmer for 15–20 minutes, until the dumplings are light and fluffy.

5 Season the stew with salt and pepper, garnish with parsley, and serve immediately while still hot.

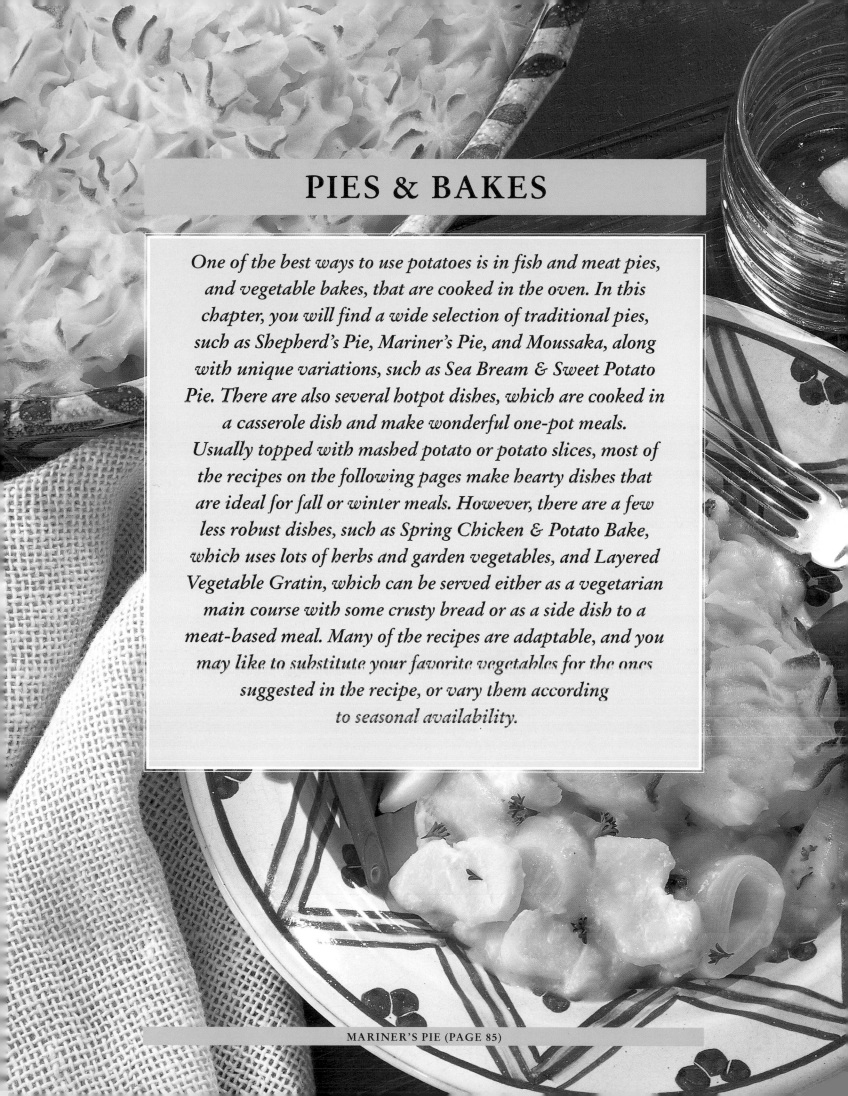

PIES & BAKES

One of the best ways to use potatoes is in fish and meat pies, and vegetable bakes, that are cooked in the oven. In this chapter, you will find a wide selection of traditional pies, such as Shepherd's Pie, Mariner's Pie, and Moussaka, along with unique variations, such as Sea Bream & Sweet Potato Pie. There are also several hotpot dishes, which are cooked in a casserole dish and make wonderful one-pot meals. Usually topped with mashed potato or potato slices, most of the recipes on the following pages make hearty dishes that are ideal for fall or winter meals. However, there are a few less robust dishes, such as Spring Chicken & Potato Bake, which uses lots of herbs and garden vegetables, and Layered Vegetable Gratin, which can be served either as a vegetarian main course with some crusty bread or as a side dish to a meat-based meal. Many of the recipes are adaptable, and you may like to substitute your favorite vegetables for the ones suggested in the recipe, or vary them according to seasonal availability.

MARINER'S PIE (PAGE 85)

OCEAN PIE

This tasty fish pie combines a mixture of fish and shellfish. You can use a wide variety of fish – whatever is easily available to you.

SERVES 4

INGREDIENTS:
*1 pound cod or haddock fillet,
  skinned
8-ounce salmon steak
scant 2 cups milk
1 bay leaf
2 pounds potatoes,
  peeled
⅓ cup peeled shrimp, thawed
  if frozen
⅓ cup butter or margarine
4 tbsp all-purpose flour
2–4 tbsp white wine
1 tsp chopped fresh dill, or ½ tsp
  dried dill
2 tbsp drained capers
salt and pepper
few whole shrimp in their shells, to
  garnish*

1 ▼ Put the cod or haddock and the salmon into a saucepan with 1¼ cups of the milk, the bay leaf, and seasoning. Bring to a boil, cover, and simmer gently for 10–15 minutes, until tender.

2 Meanwhile, coarsely chop the potatoes and cook in boiling, salted water until tender.

3 ▼ Drain the fish from the saucepan, reserving 1¼ cups of the cooking liquid (make up with more milk if necessary). Flake the fish, discarding any bones, and place in a shallow ovenproof dish. Add the shrimp.

4 Melt half the butter or margarine in a saucepan and add the flour. Cook, stirring, for a minute or so. Gradually stir in the reserved stock and the wine, and bring to a boil. Add the herbs, capers, and seasoning to taste, and simmer until thickened. Pour over the fish and mix well.

5 Drain the potatoes and mash them, adding the remaining butter or margarine, seasoning, and enough milk to give the potatoes a smooth consistency suitable for piping.

6 ▲ Put the mashed potato into a pastry bag fitted with a large star piping tip and pipe whirls over the fish to cover completely.

7 Cook in a preheated oven at 400°F for about 25 minutes, until piping hot and browned. Serve garnished with whole shrimp.

MARINER'S PIE

Make this cheap and cheerful fish pie with cod, pollock, or any inexpensive white fish.

SERVES 4

INGREDIENTS:
1½ pounds potatoes
2 large leeks, sliced
1¼ cups plus 2 tbsp milk
1 tbsp chopped fresh parsley
¼ cup butter
½ cup all-purpose flour
*1½ pounds skinned and boned white
    fish, cut into chunks*
1 egg
salt and pepper
*chopped fresh parsley,
    to garnish*

TO SERVE:
green beans
tomatoes

1 Boil the potatoes in lightly salted water for about 15 minutes, until tender. Meanwhile, cook the leeks in lightly salted, boiling water for about 8 minutes.

2 ▼ Drain the potatoes and leeks, reserving the cooking liquid. Mash the potatoes with 2 tablespoons of the milk and half the butter. Make the remaining milk up to 2½ cups with the cooking liquid from the potatoes and leeks. Add the parsley to the milk mixture.

3 ▼ Melt the remaining butter in a saucepan. Add the flour and cook gently, stirring, for 1 minute. Gradually stir in the milk and parsley mixture. Heat, stirring constantly, until thickened and smooth. Season to taste.

4 Grease a large, shallow ovenproof dish. Put the fish in the dish and arrange the cooked leeks on top.

5 ▼ Pour the parsley sauce over the fish and leeks.

6 Pipe or spoon the potatoes on top of the fish, covering completely. Bake in a preheated oven at 375°F for 25–30 minutes, until the potatoes are golden brown.

7 Garnish the pie with parsley, and serve with the beans and tomatoes.

SEA BREAM & SWEET POTATO PIE

This is a fish pie with a difference – a creamy fish sauce topped with golden sweet potatoes for a substantial supper-time meal.

SERVES 6

INGREDIENTS:
1 tbsp butter
3 tbsp peanut oil
8 ounces sweet potatoes, unpeeled and sliced thinly
1 onion, chopped finely
1½ pounds sea bream fillets, skinned and cut into large pieces
2 hard-cooked eggs, chopped
sprigs of fresh parsley,
  to garnish

CURRY SAUCE:
3 tbsp butter
2 tbsp all-purpose flour
1¼ cups milk
¾ cup grated sharp cheddar cheese
1 tsp curry powder
2 tbsp chopped fresh flat-leaf parsley
salt and pepper

1 ▼ In a large skillet, melt the butter with 2 tablespoons of the oil. Fry the sweet potatoes in batches for 1–2 minutes on each side, without letting them soften. Remove with a perforated spoon and drain on paper towels.

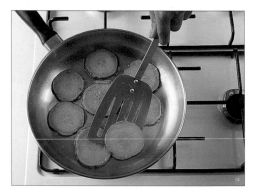

2 ▼ Add the onion to the pan and fry for 5 minutes. Add the sea bream and cook for 5 minutes more. Remove the pan from the heat and stir in the eggs. Transfer the fish mixture to an ovenproof dish.

3 To make the sauce, melt the butter in a saucepan, add the flour, and stir over a low heat for 1–2 minutes. Remove from the heat and gradually stir in the milk. Return to the heat and stir for 2–3 minutes more. Add two-thirds of the cheese, the curry powder, parsley, and seasoning.

4 ▼ Pour the sauce over the fish and mix gently. Layer the sweet potato over the top, overlapping the slices. Brush with the remaining oil and sprinkle with the remaining cheese. Bake in a preheated oven at 350°F for about 30 minutes, until golden on the top. Garnish the pie with parsley and serve hot.

SHEPHERD'S PIE

Ground lamb or beef is cooked with onions, carrots, herbs, and tomatoes, and topped with piped creamed potatoes to make a hearty and nourishing dish.

SERVES 4–5

INGREDIENTS:
*1½ pounds lean ground lamb
 or beef
2 onions, chopped
8 ounces carrots, diced
1–2 garlic cloves, crushed
1 tbsp all-purpose flour
scant 1 cup beef stock
7-ounce can chopped tomatoes
1 tsp Worcestershire sauce
1 tsp chopped fresh sage or oregano, or
 ¼ tsp dried sage or oregano
1½–2 pounds potatoes
2 tbsp butter or margarine
3–4 tbsp milk
4 ounces small mushrooms, sliced
 (optional)
salt and pepper*

1 Place the meat in a heavy based saucepan with no extra fat and cook slowly, stirring frequently, until the meat begins to brown.

2 ▼ Add the onions, carrots, and garlic, and continue to cook for about 10 minutes. Stir in the flour and cook for a minute or so, then gradually stir in the stock and tomatoes and bring to a boil.

3 ▼ Add the Worcestershire sauce, seasoning, and herbs. Cover the pan and simmer gently for about 25 minutes, giving an occasional stir.

4 Cook the potatoes in boiling, salted water until tender, then drain thoroughly and mash, beating in the butter or margarine, seasoning, and enough milk to give a consistency for piping. Place in a pastry bag fitted with a large star piping tip.

5 ▼ Stir the mushrooms, if using, into the meat and adjust the seasoning. Turn the mixture into a shallow ovenproof dish.

6 Pipe the potatoes evenly all over the meat. Cook in a preheated oven at 400°F for about 30 minutes, until piping hot and the potatoes are golden brown.

SARDINE & POTATO BAKE

Fresh sardines bear very little resemblance to the canned varieties. They are now readily available frozen, and sometimes fresh, so this traditional dish from Liguria can now be enjoyed by all.

SERVES 4

INGREDIENTS:

2 pounds potatoes, peeled
2 pounds sardines, defrosted if frozen
1 tbsp olive oil, plus extra for oiling
1 onion, peeled and chopped
2–3 garlic cloves, crushed
2 tbsp freshly chopped parsley
12 ounces ripe tomatoes, peeled and sliced, or a 15-ounce can peeled tomatoes, partly drained and chopped
1–2 tbsp freshly chopped Italian herbs, such as oregano, thyme, rosemary, and marjoram
⅔ cup dry white wine
salt and pepper

1 Put the potatoes in a saucepan of salted water, bring to a boil, cover, and simmer for 10 minutes. Drain well and let cool. When cool enough to handle, cut the potatoes into slices about ¼-inch thick.

2 ▲ Gut and clean the sardines. Cut off their heads and tails, and then slit open the length of the belly. Turn the fish over so the skin side is up, and press firmly along the backbone to loosen the bones. Turn over again and carefully remove the backbone. Wash the fish in cold water, drain well, and dry them on paper towels.

3 Heat the oil in a skillet, and fry the onion and garlic until soft, but not colored.

4 ▼ Arrange the potatoes in a well-oiled ovenproof dish and sprinkle with the onions. Scatter the parsley on top and add plenty of seasoning.

5 ▼ Lay the open sardines over the potatoes, skin-side down, then cover with the tomatoes and the rest of the herbs. Pour on the wine and season.

6 Cook, uncovered, in a preheated oven at 375°F for about 40 minutes, until the fish is tender. If the casserole seems to be drying out, add another couple of tablespoons of wine.

LAYERED VEGETABLE GRATIN

The word "gratin" usually describes a baked crust made from eggs and flour. In this recipe, an assortment of vegetables are cooked in a light nutmeg sauce with a potato and cheese topping. The gratin makes a great vegetarian main course, but can also be served as an accompaniment.

SERVES 6

INGREDIENTS:
2 large carrots
8 ounces baby parsnips
1 whole Florence fennel
  bulb
3 potatoes
¼ cup low-fat spread
¼ cup all-purpose flour
1¼ cups skimmed milk
½ tsp ground nutmeg
1 egg, beaten
¼ cup freshly grated Parmesan
  cheese
salt and pepper

TO SERVE:
crusty bread
mixed salad

1 ▼ Cut the carrots and parsnips into thin lengthwise strips. Cook in boiling water for 5 minutes. Drain well and transfer to an ovenproof baking dish.

2 Thinly slice the fennel and cook in boiling water for 2–3 minutes. Drain well, and add to the carrots and parsnips. Season.

3 ▲ Peel and dice the potatoes into ¾-inch cubes. Cook in boiling water for 6 minutes. Drain the potatoes well and set aside.

4 Gently melt half the low-fat spread in a saucepan and stir in the flour. Remove from the heat and gradually mix in the milk. Return to the heat and stir until thickened. Season and stir in the nutmeg. Let the mixture cool for 10 minutes.

5 ▼ Beat in the egg and spoon the mixture over the vegetables. Arrange the potatoes on top and sprinkle over the grated cheese. Dot with the remaining low-fat spread.

6 Bake in a preheated oven at 350°F for 1 hour, until the vegetables are tender.

7 Serve hot with crusty bread and a mixed salad.

SCALLOPED POTATOES

Layers of sliced potatoes with onions and diced bacon are topped with crispy browned cheese. This dish can be cooked with stock for everyday meals, or with cream if you want to make it more special.

SERVES 4

INGREDIENTS:
2¼ pounds potatoes
2 large onions, chopped finely
2 garlic cloves, crushed
   (optional)
6–8 ounces lean bacon,
   diced
2 tbsp chopped fresh dill, or
   ¼ tsp dried dill
scant 2 cups stock, milk, or light
   cream
1 tbsp butter or margarine,
   melted
¼ cup grated sharp cheddar, Gouda, or
   Emmentaler cheese
salt and pepper

1 Slice the potatoes, either by hand or using a food processor.

2 ▲ Grease a large ovenproof dish or roasting pan well. Arrange a layer of sliced potatoes in the dish or pan and sprinkle with half the onions. Season lightly.

3 ▼ Add a second layer of potatoes, then the rest of the onions, the garlic, if using, the bacon, dill, and seasoning, sprinkling evenly. Add a final layer of potatoes, arranging them in an attractive pattern.

4 Gently heat the stock, milk, or cream and pour over the potatoes. Brush the top layer of potatoes with the melted butter or margarine, and cover with greased foil or a lid.

5 Bake the potatoes in a preheated oven at 400°F for about 1 hour.

6 ▼ Remove the foil or lid, and sprinkle the cheese over the potatoes.

7 Return the dish, uncovered, to the oven for 30–45 minutes more, until the cheese is well browned on top and the potatoes are tender. Serve immediately while still hot.

SAVORY HOTPOT

This hearty lamb stew is full of vegetables and herbs, and topped with a layer of crisp, golden potato slices.

SERVES 4

INGREDIENTS:
8 middle neck lamb chops, neck of lamb, or any stewing lamb on the bone
1–2 garlic cloves, crushed
2 lamb's kidneys (optional)
1 large onion, sliced thinly
1 leek, sliced
2–3 carrots, sliced
1 tsp chopped fresh tarragon or sage, or ½ tsp dried tarragon or sage
2 pounds potatoes, sliced thinly
1¼ cups stock
32 tbsp butter or margarine, melted, or 1 tbsp vegetable oil
salt and pepper
chopped fresh parsley, to garnish

1 ▼ Trim the lamb of any excess fat, season well with salt and pepper, and arrange in a large ovenproof casserole. Sprinkle with the garlic.

2 If using kidneys, remove the skin, halve the kidneys, and cut out the cores. Chop into small pieces and sprinkle over the lamb.

3 ▲ Place the onion, leek, and carrots over the lamb, letting the pieces slip in between the meat, then sprinkle with the herbs.

4 Arrange the potato slices evenly and overlapping over the contents of the casserole.

5 Bring the stock to a boil, season with salt and pepper, then pour over the casserole.

6 ▼ Brush the potatoes with melted butter or margarine, or oil, cover with greased foil or a lid, and cook in a preheated oven at 350°F for about 1½ hours.

7 Remove the foil or lid from the potatoes, increase the oven temperature to 425°F, and return the casserole to the oven for about 30 minutes, until the potatoes are browned. Garnish with chopped parsley and serve.

BACON, ONION, & POTATO HOTPOT

Simple, straightforward, and satisfying, this warming casserole is perfect for chilly winter days.

SERVES 4

INGREDIENTS:
¼ cup butter or margarine
2 pounds main crop potatoes, sliced
1 pound onions, sliced
3½ cups chicken stock
1 pound bacon
salt and pepper
steamed broccoli, to serve

1 ▼ Grease a 2-quart casserole dish with some of the butter or margarine. Layer the potatoes and onions alternately in the casserole dish, seasoning each layer. Finish with a layer of potatoes.

2 ▼ Pour the stock over the potatoes and dot the surface with the remaining butter or margarine. Cover and bake in a preheated oven at 375°F for 45 minutes.

3 ▼ Remove the lid from the casserole and return to the oven for 30 minutes more, until the potatoes are golden brown.

4 Meanwhile, cook the bacon under a preheated moderately hot broiler, until cooked, but not too crisp.

5 ▲ Put the bacon on top of the potatoes and cook in the oven for 10 minutes longer. Serve at once on warm plates, with the cooked broccoli.

LAMB & POTATO MOUSSAKA

Ground lamb makes a very tasty and authentic moussaka. For a change, use ground beef.

SERVES 4

INGREDIENTS:
1 large eggplant, sliced
1 tbsp olive or vegetable oil
1 onion, chopped finely
1 garlic clove, crushed
12 ounces ground lamb
8 ounces mushrooms, sliced
14-ounce can chopped tomatoes with herbs
⅔ cup lamb or vegetable stock
2 tbsp cornstarch
2 tbsp water
1 pound potatoes, parboiled for 10 minutes and sliced
2 eggs
½ cup low-fat cream cheese
⅔ cup plain yogurt
½ cup grated sharp cheddar cheese
salt and pepper
fresh flat-leaf parsley, to garnish
green salad, to serve

1 ▼ Lay the eggplant slices on a clean work counter and sprinkle liberally with salt, to extract the bitter juices. Leave for 10 minutes, then turn the slices over and repeat. Put in a colander, rinse, and drain well.

2 ▲ Meanwhile, heat the oil in a saucepan, and fry the onion and garlic for 3–4 minutes. Add the lamb and mushrooms, and cook for 5 minutes, until browned. Stir in the tomatoes and stock, bring to a boil, and simmer for 10 minutes. Mix the cornstarch with the water and stir it into the saucepan. Cook, stirring, until thickened.

3 Spoon half the mixture into an ovenproof dish. Cover with the eggplant slices, then the remaining lamb mixture. Arrange the sliced potatoes on top.

4 ▼ Beat together the eggs, cream cheese, yogurt, and seasoning. Pour over the potatoes to cover them completely. Sprinkle with the grated cheese.

5 Bake in a preheated oven at 375°F for 45 minutes, until the topping is set and golden brown. Garnish with the flat-leaf parsley and serve accompanied by a green salad.

SPRING CHICKEN & POTATO BAKE

Make this delicious dish when new potatoes are in season. A medium onion or a few shallots can be substituted for the scallions in the recipe.

SERVES 4

INGREDIENTS:

2 tbsp olive oil
4 chicken breasts
1 bunch scallions, trimmed and
   chopped
12 ounces young spring carrots,
   scrubbed and sliced
4 ounces dwarf green beans, trimmed
   and sliced
2¼ cups chicken stock
12 ounces small new potatoes,
   scrubbed
1 small bunch mixed fresh herbs, such
   as thyme, rosemary, bay, and parsley
salt and pepper
2 tbsp cornstarch
2–3 tbsp cold water
sprigs of fresh mixed herbs, to garnish

1 Heat the oil in a large flameproof casserole dish and add the chicken breasts. Gently fry for 5–8 minutes, until browned on both sides. Lift from the casserole with a perforated spoon and set aside.

2 ▲ Add the scallions, carrots, and green beans, and gently fry for 3–4 minutes.

3 ▼ Return the chicken breasts to the casserole and pour in the chicken stock. Add the potatoes and herbs. Season with salt and pepper. Bring to a boil, then cover the casserole and transfer to the oven. Bake in a preheated oven at 375°F for 40–50 minutes, until the potatoes are tender.

4 ▲ Blend the cornstarch with the cold water. Add to the casserole, stirring until blended and thickened. Cover and cook for 5 minutes longer. Garnish with fresh herbs and serve.

BEEF PIE WITH RED CABBAGE

*This stew of slow-cooked braising
steak with onions and potatoes is
topped with a pie dough and served
with pickled red cabbage.
A deep casserole dish works best
for this pie.*

SERVES 4

INGREDIENTS:
2 tbsp vegetable oil
*1½ pounds braising steak, trimmed and
  cubed*
3¼ cups beef stock
2 medium onions, chopped
*2 pounds potatoes, peeled and
  cubed*
salt and pepper
pickled red cabbage, to serve

PIE DOUGH:
2 cups all-purpose flour
¼ tsp salt
¼ cup margarine
6–7 tbsp chilled water
milk, for brushing

1 ▼ Heat the vegetable oil in a large
saucepan. Add the beef and fry over a
high heat for 5–8 minutes, until
browned on all sides. Add the stock.
Bring to a boil, then cover and reduce
the heat. Simmer for 1½ hours, until
the meat is tender.

2 Add the onions and potatoes. Bring
back to a boil, then reduce the heat
and simmer, uncovered, for about
20 minutes, until the potatoes are
tender. Season to taste.

3 Transfer the meat and potato mixture
to a 2-quart casserole dish and leave to
cool slightly.

4 ▼ Meanwhile make the pie dough.
Sift the flour and salt into a bowl. Cut
the margarine into pieces and add to
the bowl. Cut in until the mixture
resembles fine bread crumbs. Add
enough chilled water to make a soft,
but not sticky, dough. Knead the
dough lightly for a few seconds until
it is smooth.

5 ▼ Roll out the dough on a lightly
floured work counter to fit the top of
the casserole dish. Make a small hole
in the middle so steam can escape.

6 Lift the dough onto the top of the
casserole and pinch the edges to seal,
trimming off any extra. Brush with a
little milk. Stand on a baking sheet and
bake in a preheated oven at 400°F for
25–30 minutes, until the pastry is
cooked and golden. Serve with the
pickled red cabbage.

INDEX